THE

TRANSCENDENTAL MEDITATION TECHNIQUE

AND

THE JOURNEY

OF

ENLIGHTENMENT

THE

TRANSCENDENTAL MEDITATION
TECHNIQUE

AND

THE JOURNEY

OF

ENLIGHTENMENT

ANN PURCELL

The Transcendental Meditation technique and the Journey of Enlightenment

©2015 Green Dragon Books
Second Edition

First Edition ©2012 Ann Purcell
Let Your Soul Sing: Enlightenment is for Everyone

Green Dragon Publishing
P.O. Box 1608
Lake Worth, FL 33460
http://www.greendragonbooks.com

Printed in the United States of America and the United Kingdom

ISBN (Paperback) 978-1-62386-020-2

Library of Congress Cataloging-in-Publication Data Control # 2014954206

DEDICATION

This book is dedicated to
His Holiness
Maharishi Mahesh Yogi
in appreciation for his offering to the world
the possibility to live a life in growing
enlightenment
through the practice of
Transcendental Meditation®
and the Transcendental Meditation Sidhi ProgramSM

TABLE OF CONTENTS

ACKNOWLEDGEMENTS

I did not plan to write a book, nor did I ever think I was even capable of writing one. One day while I was home I started to write down a short little story as a gift for my sister. Every night when I went to bed a flood of thoughts came into my mind, which I wrote down the next day. This went on for about two months, and before I knew it, there was the first draft of a whole book! I showed it to a few friends and family and they liked it and thought it was worth developing.

A very dear and brilliant friend of mine, whom I have worked closely with in the Transcendental Meditation organization since 1974, read the draft, really liked it, and offered to edit it. As soon as she offered to edit it, I knew that this book would become a reality. In addition to editing and polishing the grammar, she encouraged me to clarify, elaborate, and rewrite many of the ideas in the book.

Close family friends, including Heather Frazer and a few other excellent editors, also took the time to go through the book and offer their suggestions. I would like to express my deepest appreciation to all these dear friends who contributed their editing skills, encouragement, and support, propelling this book into completion.

I also want to thank my family, especially my mother, for their ongoing flexibility and support.

INTRODUCTION

When I was 12 years old, I received my first guitar for Christmas. One day I was sitting outside by the pool trying to play it when Percy, our gardener, walked up to me.

"Gimme that guitar, girl," Percy said.

I handed my guitar to Percy and he started playing a blues riff. Then he started singing. I was stunned. Out came this soft, smooth, honey-toned voice. I felt a tender wave inside. My heart began to melt. This is the first memory I have of a real inner feeling being enlivened, my first memory of "inside."

Percy was the son of Arthur "Big Boy" Crudup, who was a blues singer from the south. Arthur Crudup wrote the song, "That's All Right, Mama," which Elvis Presley made famous.

When my sister and I were playing and singing together, whenever we saw Percy we would ask him to sing for us. Percy knew how to sing from the feeling level; he knew how to let his soul sing.

I have a soft, high-pitched little girl's voice, but my younger sister has a gravelly low-pitched Louis Armstrong-type voice. She can really belt out the blues. She and Percy would sing together sometimes. It was an unusual duo—a young teenage girl and the forty-something family gardener. Wow, were they a team! Somehow their voices really blended.

When they sang together, I always felt a surge of joy in my heart. My body would automatically start swaying and my hands would begin clapping. My sister and Percy used to joke, although with a hint of seriousness, that one day they were going to go on the road together and become famous, but life took them both in other directions. My sister got married and had two wonderful children, and Percy became the head of the shipping department of my family's company. Years later, Percy came down with cancer and had to have his voice box removed; fortunately, this did not dampen his spirit, and he maintained his wonderful joy of life until his passing a few years ago.

My love for music continued. I would sit in my room for hours listening to all my records, and I practiced on my guitar but never had the voice to be a good singer. When I went to prep school, I wanted to be part of the singing groups, but I never even bothered to try out since the singers in those groups were so good.

Although I always wished I had a really good singing voice, maybe then my life would not have taken the wonderful direction it did. During my first year of college, I started on an unexpected spiritual journey. This turn in my life was completely divergent from the road I had been traveling thus far. Fortunately, this unpredicted path my life took taught me how to truly let my soul sing from deep within.

1
COMING HOME

"This is the glory of the nature of the Self. Having come back home, the traveler finds peace. The intensity of happiness is beyond the superlative. The bliss of this state eliminates the possibility of any sorrow, great or small. . . . This state of self-sufficiency leaves one steadfast in oneself, fulfilled in eternal contentment."[1]

—Maharishi

I had a wonderful upbringing—winters in Florida, summers on the New England coast. My parents really enjoyed life, they were always there for me, and life seemed to be one big party. I barely escaped the pitfalls of the sixties and was relatively unscarred by teenage escapades. One day, when I was eighteen years old and in my first year of college, my life took an unexpected turn.

A friend of mine was going to a college in England that her father's friend had started. She asked me to go with her, and I thought it would be an exciting adventure to go to school in Europe. I ended up in a quaint and charming village in the Cotswolds at a little college outside of Oxford, called Alvescot College. There were only twelve other students there, none of whom I had anything in common with. Therefore, I was looking around for something to get involved in so that I could meet other people and one day I read the brochure, "What's On in Oxford." It was mostly about the various Shakespeare plays and concerts taking place in town. The brochure also advertised different lectures that were being held in the area, including a lecture on Transcendental Meditation (TM®).

On a whim, I went and was very impressed with the TM teacher who was giving the lecture. She had a very calm, easy nature about her, and everything she said made sense. I decided to take the course.

I'll never forget my first meditation. I felt so still and peaceful, yet I felt a heightened alertness as well. It was probably the longest I had ever sat still—quiet and settled—in my whole life; it was only 20 minutes! Afterwards, I felt a huge weight had been lifted from me. It dawned on me that I had found something I had been looking for my whole life without even knowing I was searching for something. Immediately I knew I had come home.

Up to this point my whole life had been social. I was always surrounded by people; rarely was I ever able to be alone unless I was reading a book or watching TV. I thought it was amazing that I could sit by myself and meditate and actually enjoy it. It seemed like a miracle.

Over the next months, I noticed many changes taking place within me. First of all, I began to focus on my schoolwork. I was the type of student who only did well if I liked my teacher and the course. I was quite an expert at getting out of homework or doing just the bare minimum to pass. I was definitely someone who slipped through the cracks as far as my high school education was concerned. I am sure I must have had ADD— attention deficit disorder—because I felt so restless in class and always avoided doing my homework. After learning Transcendental Meditation, I started regularly going to the library in Oxford to study. I loved the silence and would stay for hours. Believe me, this was a dramatic change!

I also noticed that I started to become more aware of my surroundings, especially of nature. The outdoors took on a vibrant transparency, and I began to notice details and textures in the leaves, grass, and trees. The sweet fragrance of flowers became more apparent. The freshness after a gentle rainfall enlivened all of my senses. I began to feel connected with my environment and, most of all, I felt the beauty of nature stir my emotions. Something inside me started to sing with the joy of life. My soul began to sing from within itself.

The following poem by the 13th century Sufi master, Hafiz, expresses my experience of transcendental Being waking up inside me:

> What is this precious love and laughter
> Budding in our hearts?
> It is the glorious sound
> Of a soul waking up! [2]

Another change I noticed was that I began to feel at home—more comfortable and natural—in any situation, because I was feeling more at home with my Self.

My own experience is universally expressed in a poem, "TM is a Place That We Call Home," written by a fifth grade girl from the Ideal Academy Public Charter School in Washington D.C., where all the students practice Transcendental Meditation. The words speak for themselves:

TM is a Place That We Call Home

When you're feeling blue
And you don't know what to do
Just slow it down a bit
Get comfortable and sit

When you close your eyes
And you go deep inside
And when you know you're done
Everything feels so right

When you're feeling sad
And you're feeling all alone
That is when TM
Is a place that we call home

When you're feeling sad
And you're feeling all alone
That is when TM
Is a place that we call home

When you're under stress
Then all you have to do
Is take a mental rest
Cause it will help you through

You may feel some rest
Or maybe energized
But either way you know
It's nice to feel at home

When you're feeling sad
And you're feeling all alone
That is when TM
Is a place that we call home

When you're feeling sad
And you're feeling all alone
That is when TM
Is a place that we call home

—Ife Calhoun, Washington, D.C.

In a poem I wrote years after learning TM, I recalled that early
experience of "coming home."

Coming Home

The first time I transcended
I had finally come home.
My long search suddenly ended
walking down many long roads.

My home is a silent place—
a dark vast vibrant sphere.
A place that everyday I embrace,
its warm security beyond fear.

With time I began to explore
the different sparkling rooms
and sank deeper into a crystal core,
sweet like roses in bloom.

Now I own this cosmic dwelling
as my universal, divine abode.
Here love is ever swelling
within itself, love continually unfolds.

Everywhere is now my home,
as my silent Self is everywhere.
I feel blessed in this sacred dome
in which every breath is a prayer.

2

THE INWARD JOURNEY –
TRANSCENDENTAL CONSCIOUSNESS

"You are divine inside, you are cosmic inside, you are universal inside. Your soul is a unified field. You are bliss inside, you are a flow of bliss, you are a flow of total natural law. You are invincible, you are powerful, you are integrated."[1]

—Maharishi

Before I learned Transcendental Meditation, my life was moving in a horizontal direction—from event to event. It was a crazy time characterized by the Vietnam War protests, the Sixties' anti-establishment culture, but also by tremendous openings in the fields of music and art. When I started meditating my life took a vertical direction, and my inward journey began. Magical events and exciting unexpected turns on the road occurred. I was now on a smooth, yet thrilling, jet plane of evolution, no longer drifting on a slow rocky boat.

After a year of meditating, I decided to attend the TM teacher training course being held in Switzerland in 1973. Being a full-time teacher of Transcendental Meditation for over 35 years has been extremely rewarding. Although I would enjoy chronicling my memories of teaching TM around the world, my purpose in writing this book is to describe the growth of consciousness that has developed inwardly and outwardly as a result of my practice of Transcendental Meditation.

Although everyone's experiences on a spiritual path are very personal and unique, the ongoing changes I have come to enjoy are very similar to the experiences of millions of people around the world practicing Transcendental Meditation and its advanced techniques. In describing my own experiences, I am only mirroring the inner journey of countless others who are experiencing the natural growth of consciousness. These universal experiences reveal that higher states of consciousness—enlightenment—can be systematically developed by anyone through the regular experience of transcendental consciousness. I will include some of these experiences from many different meditators at the end of each chapter, and will share my own experiences mostly in the form of poems.

In order to have a framework to understand higher states of consciousness, the first essential question to ask is, "What is consciousness?"

Our awareness, perceptions, feelings, ideas, imaginations, and thoughts are all expressions of our consciousness. How clear, or awake, our consciousness is can vary from day to day. We all know what it's like when we haven't slept well. The next morning our awareness is dull and restricted. We tend to make mistakes and are easily irritated by others. Compare that to the experience of waking up refreshed after a good night's sleep. Everything looks brighter; we meet challenges with new insights and understanding. Our thinking is orderly, compassionate, and creative when our consciousness is clear and refreshed.

The quieter, subtler levels of consciousness are teeming with energy, intelligence, and creativity. The subtlest level, transcendental consciousness, is beyond the field of thought and is the most silent level of our Being— an unbounded state of inner wakefulness—pure consciousness.

The next question we need to ask is, "What is Transcendental Meditation?"

Transcendental Meditation is a simple, natural, mental technique, practiced sitting comfortably with eyes closed. During the practice, the mind settles down effortlessly to quieter levels of thought until the quietest, most refined level of thinking is transcended and you experience the field of unbounded awareness—transcendental consciousness. In this state, you are left alone with your Self—the big Self, the Knower, the Experiencer, the absolutely deepest level of your Being. When you experience your deepest Self, you will know for certain that you are infinite, boundless, eternal—a limitless reservoir of energy, intelligence, and bliss.

The mind and body are intimately connected, so as the mind settles down to this quiet level of pure consciousness, the body also gains a unique state of deep rest. This deep rest dissolves stress and fatigue. Transcendental Meditation does not involve effort or concentration and does not require any change in belief or lifestyle. Over five million people around the world of all cultures, religions, and educational backgrounds have learned Transcendental Meditation (TM) in the past 50 years.

His Holiness Maharishi Mahesh Yogi brought Transcendental Meditation to the West in 1958. Before coming to the West, Maharishi lived a reclusive life in India for fourteen years in the service of his teacher, Brahmananda Saraswati, Shankaracharya of Jyotir Math, known as Guru Dev. After Guru Dev's passing, Maharishi retired to a cave in Uttar Kashi, high in the Himalayas. After about two years, a recurring thought arose in him to travel to Rameshvaram in the south of India. To the recluses of Uttar Kashi, such an idea of leaving the deep silence and spiritual atmosphere of this ideal hermitage and going out into the relentlessly chaotic world was unthinkable! When the thought continued to come up for nearly a year, Maharishi finally mentioned it to a wise saint, who responded: "I think you have been thinking of it for so long. Why not get rid of this thought[?]"[2] Maharishi explained that the saint's words "get rid of this thought" meant, "go there and come back and never think of it again."

Maharishi agreed and traveled to Rameshvaram, planning to stay only for a short time and then return to the Himalayas. He later recalled that after some time in Rameshvaram, another thought came: why not give the wisdom of the Himalayas to the people of south India?

Coming from the Himalayas, I had the thought—it was very fresh in my mind—that it is not necessary for man to suffer. All the literature in India is full of beautiful exaltations. The Vedas say, 'Amritasya putra'—'O sons of immortality!'— addressing all mankind as sons of immortality. The Vedas say, 'Of ananda [bliss] all this is born, in ananda all this is sustained, and to ananda all this is going.[3]

But where is the reality of this in the day-to-day life of the people? There is such a gap between what life is declared to be and what life is found to be. Experiencing that unboundedness, the source of all creation, that immortality, and living that in life, is such a simple thing. I was so naturally and deeply moved between the two realities: life being lived on a completely wretched level and life described on the most exalted level. There was no connection between the two. And there was no reason why there should be a gap, because it's so simple for the individual to be on that level of universality and immortality. It's so simple. This was the natural feeling that was deep in my mind, that something should be done so that people don't suffer, because there is no reason to suffer....[4]

While traveling in the south of India, Maharishi started teaching the technique of Transcendental Meditation to the people who flocked to him. He was met with such an enthusiastic response that he spent the next two years traveling all over India teaching TM. In 1957 in Madras, India, in honor of Guru Dev's birthday, Maharishi held a three-day "Spiritual Luminaries Seminar." At this festival, he inaugurated the Spiritual Regeneration Movement to spiritually regenerate the whole world.

To reach the entire world's population, Maharishi decided to travel to the west, where communication was more efficient. Along the way, he taught Transcendental Meditation to all who came. In 1958 he arrived for the first time in the United States.

Maharishi brought out a very simple philosophy of life: the purpose of life is the expansion of happiness, life is here to enjoy, and no one has the right to suffer. Transcendental Meditation was the practical technique he offered for everyone to develop and enjoy this state of life. Maharishi himself fully embodied his message, and everywhere he went people were drawn to his serene, joyful presence.

It is impossible to describe Maharishi's profoundly calm and silent demeanor, his bubbling blissful personality, and the unprecedented wisdom he unfolded in over twenty thousand hours of videotaped recordings of his lectures, and in the many books he wrote, including *The Science of Being and Art of Living* and his translation and commentary on the Bhagavad-Gita. He established many universities around the world, including Maharishi University of Management in Fairfield, Iowa, which offers degree programs through the doctoral level and is accredited by the Higher Learning Commission.

Maharishi worked tirelessly, virtually non-stop for over 50 years (often twenty hours a day!), never wavering even one second from his goal of bringing Transcendental Meditation and its advanced technologies to the entire world. He developed a detailed practical plan to create world peace, ideal government, global affluence, and a world free from problems and suffering, which he called nothing less than Heaven on Earth. I believe that soon the world will come to appreciate the depth and breadth of Maharishi's teaching and plans for a beautiful, ideal world.

With the worldwide introduction of Transcendental Meditation, Maharishi offered a universally simple, natural, and above all, effective technique that can be practiced by anyone and that produces immediate results. This stands in contrast to the conventional view of meditation, which has often been considered a difficult process, requiring a great ability to concentrate and involving a lot of effort and strain.

There are many types of meditation available today. These include mindfulness, or trying to be present with whatever happens; concentration, or holding on to some thought or visualization; and those in which the practitioner tries to empty the mind and find stillness. It is important to understand that Transcendental Meditation is different from all these types of meditations. It is effortless and completely natural. Anyone can learn, and in the very first meditation, one spontaneously settles to a level of deep silence. This practice is easily learned. Children can learn starting from the age of ten.

Although Transcendental Meditation is completely easy and natural to practice, one cannot learn the technique from a book, a DVD, or from someone else who has learned but is not a certified teacher. Anyone who learns the Transcendental Meditation technique is always taught by a certified instructor who has gone through several months of in-residence training.

The standardized course of instruction involves seven steps: two introductory lectures, a personal interview, then four teaching sessions over four consecutive days, each lasting about an hour and a half. After completing the seven-lesson course, you are encouraged to have your meditation checked once a month for the next few months, in order to ensure the effortlessness of the experience and to answer any questions that may arise.

When I read the popular *NY Times* bestseller *Eat, Pray, Love,* I felt very sorry for Elizabeth Gilbert as she described her experience of meditating in an ashram in India. It seemed almost painful for her to sit and try to meditate since she was so restless and uncomfortable. Fortunately, she finally did have a breakthrough and some positive experiences, but all that trying and discomfort was so unnecessary.

The transcendent—Being—pure consciousness, stillness—is the inner essence of everyone, so to experience it is the most natural thing in the world. One only needs a technique to dive within in order to experience it daily. Even without a meditation technique, many philosophers, poets, saints, athletes, and people from all walks of life and religious backgrounds have on occasion spontaneously enjoyed the experience of transcendental consciousness and described it in their own words.

Just as the ability to walk is inherent in the ability to run, and the ability to stand still is inherent in the ability to walk, so the mind has the ability to be more active, less active, and completely still. The only thing missing is simply the technique for anyone to experience that silence regularly.

Many poets throughout history have expressed the natural experience of transcendence, or pure consciousness. I particularly love Emily Dickinson's poem "There is a solitude of space,"

> There is a solitude of space,
> A solitude of sea,
> A solitude of death, but these
> Society shall be,
> Compared with that profounder site,
> That polar privacy,
> A Soul admitted to itself:
> Finite Infinity.[5]

Henry David Thoreau, the American Transcendentalist, beautifully described what we are missing in his "meditation" on meditation:

> If with closed ears and eyes I consult consciousness for a moment, immediately are all walls and barriers dissipated, earth rolls from under me, and I float . . . in the midst of an unknown and infinite sea . . .[6] We become like a still lake of purest crystal and without an effort our depths are revealed to ourselves.[7]

Eugene Ionesco, the great Romanian/French playwright and dramatist, described his experience of the transcendent:

> I suddenly entered the heart of a reality
> so blindingly obvious, so total, so enlightening,
> so luminous, that I wondered how I had never
> before realized how easy this reality was to find
> and how easily I found myself in it . . .
> This state of supernormal wakefulness could set
> the world ablaze, transfigure it, illuminate it.[8]

Here is another profound poem by Emily Dickinson about the cosmic nature of the brain:

> The Brain is wider than the Sky,
> For, put them side by side
> The one the other will include
> With ease, and you beside.

The brain is deeper than the sea,
For, hold them, blue to blue,
The one the other will absorb,
As sponges, buckets do.[9]

There are also many accounts of athletes who have had transcendental experiences even during an athletic performance. The tennis champion Billy Jean King said when describing a perfect shot, "I can almost feel it coming.... I am able to transport myself beyond the turmoil on the court to some place of total peace and calm."[10]

Steve McKinney, a pro skier, experienced something similar when he broke the world downhill ski record: "I discovered the middle path of stillness within speed, calmness within fear, and I held it longer and quieter than ever before."[11]

Shoshin Nagamine describes the experience of karate:

The fusing of mind and body in karate is indescribably beautiful. The flow of the mind, when totally absorbed during kata practice [a series of Japanese moves and choreography in karate], brings a person into contact with the essence and core of his being. One is both humbled and uplifted by this knowledge of Self.[12]

The wise seer of China—Lao Tzu—clearly had experiences of transcendence that are brought to light in his teachings, which include books called *Wenzi* and the *Tao te Ching.* Throughout his works, Lao Tzu asserts that the most important thing people can do in life is to gain a state of silent awareness—to open the mind to its source:

The superior person settles his mind as the universe settles the stars in the sky. By connecting the mind with the subtle origin, he calms it. Once calmed it naturally expands, and ultimately his mind becomes as vast and immeasurable as the night sky.

...

Remain quiet. Discover the harmony in your own being. Embrace it. If you can do this, you will gain everything, and the world will become healthy again. If you can't, you will be lost in the shadows forever.[13]

...

To the mind that is still the whole Universe surrenders.

Lao Tzu called this universal field of life the *Tao*, or *Dao*, which is often translated as "the Way," or "the Path."

When one practices the Transcendental Meditation technique and has the experience of transcendence, along with the understanding of Maharishi's teaching about consciousness, it becomes obvious that Lao Tzu is talking about transcending. Many people who practice the Transcendental Meditation technique have had experiences just as he describes. It's amazing to think that even though he lived in the 5th century B.C.—2,600 years ago—he had the same experiences that so many individuals are enjoying in the 21st century around the world. This verifies that these are universal experiences beyond time, space, and culture.

Experiences of the transcendent can come spontaneously at any moment. There are many accounts of saints having one or two very profound experiences of transcendence, sometimes while praying. The experience is so profound and overwhelming that they spend the rest of their life trying to regain that experience. The beauty and profundity of the Transcendental Meditation technique is that you can experience the transcendent even in your first meditation and daily deepen that experience, which grows fuller and richer over time.

During the first few years after I started meditating, the experience of deep silence was absorbing and charming. I would see a dark vastness in front of me. In time this darkness sometimes transformed into a field of brilliant light. The experience was one of increasing pleasantness. I felt anchored to my inner depths, less tossed about by outer changing circumstances. Underlying insecurities started to dissolve, and I felt stronger and more accepting of myself as a person.

Life became increasingly alive—vibrant—and I started to live more and more in the present. My mind was no longer bogged down by thousands of thoughts and anxieties, and there was clearer direction, clarity, and focus in whatever I was doing. I also felt that activity was increasingly effortless. My life started to flow like a gentle river.

I would like to share a poem I wrote called "Tender Flower of Heaven" about my first experiences of meeting the transcendental, silent level of life.

Tender Flower of Heaven

The first moment I touched you —
  my own stillness—
I experienced a certainty—
  a deep, vast fullness—
that I never knew before;
  a peaceful rest
 in softness of my Self
  that compressed
life's purpose into this moment,
  and impressed
on me life's true meaning.
  I coalesced
with purest love that exists,
  and repossessed
a confidence of knowing—
  knowingness—
that now cushions my life
  in sweetness
allowing me to move free—
  unoppressed
in the calm of my Being.
  I confess
I want to sing aloud
  and address
all to experience their silence
  and access
the beauty of life—
  the gentleness—
of the tender flower of heaven.

Experiences

I felt myself descending so deep, like I was falling into this deep hole. I felt this bright spinning, it was indescribable—a beautiful feeling. I literally just for the longest time was in this deep, deep place all by myself and it was the most comforting feeling, I can't describe it, it was just wonderful; it was awesome. I didn't hear anything, nothing, except when the teacher told me to open my eyes. I felt a complete peace over my body, like a feeling that most people just don't feel.

G.L.—New York

When I close my eyes to meditate, it is as if I enter another world. The minutiae of everyday life seems insignificant and fades away. I am supremely at peace with myself, my life, and the world. My mind and body become crystal clear with the experience of my own true nature—pure consciousness. I am filled with bliss, a bliss that is not dependent on anything. It comes from a supremely pure center of joy that is within me.

S.D.—Canada

I didn't really have an interest in Transcendental Meditation until I was asked to try it, but I thought: I'll give it a shot, sounds interesting. I can feel the difference all the way around. Everybody has stress and anxiety but when you meditate it goes right away, and it's amazing how I can sit there and meditate and be in this deep spot yet be aware of everything around me. If I meditate in the morning my day is really great. It's hard to explain to somebody, it really is, until you do it, then you can get the whole picture. But to try to explain it to somebody, it's almost impossible.

W.L.—New York

3
TRANSFORMATIONS

"The quality of bliss pulsating in the consciousness of the artist creates expressions of bliss in his art. When art is created from this eternal field of pure consciousness, it will continue to inspire life generation after generation."[1]

—Maharishi

After about a year of practicing Transcendental Meditation, an interesting phenomenon began to occur. Out of the blue, I started hearing melodies in my head, or sometimes words and phrases started bubbling up inside. Although I had learned to play the guitar when I was a teenager, I did not consider myself to be very musical. Suddenly I was writing all these songs and poems. The songs seemed to write themselves, as though I were just a vessel for them to flow through and emerge. My silent awareness was bursting with creativity, with words and rhythms that seemed to be embedded in my soul.

Following are two poems; the first one expresses my experience of writing a poem, and the second one expresses my experience of writing a song.

Writing a Poem

I love being absorbed
    writing a poem.
I am in an orb
    or a cosmic dome
that churns round
    spinning out words
searching for the profound
    that in silence is heard.

Tender thoughtful feelings
    flowing as a stream
hopefully revealing
    an original theme.
I catch them with my pen
    as they blissfully rush forth
again, again, and again
    like a river on course.
My heart is tenderly stirred
    as the poem reveals itself,
forming phrases from words
    that appear by stealth.
I become elated,
    my spirit sweetly soars
when the flow has abated
    with no more outpour,
especially if the thought is complete
    in rhythmic dancing rhymes,
with a message that is concrete
    and meaningful for all times.

Music in Silence

Striking the tones of silence
    music gently starts to flow.
Silence is purest harmony—
    all frequencies in synchronous glow.
Self stirring this tender stillness,
    sound subtly begins to hum.
In superfluid gentle swings
    silent strings softly strum.
As Self hears its own song
    consciousness begins to dance
to the music of its own nature—
    the melody of blissful resonance.

My continued experience of deeper values of silence during Transcendental Meditation unleashed this effortless flow of creativity. The outpouring of these poems really surprised me, as I never aspired in any way to be a poet or a songwriter. Everyone has an ocean of creativity inside; we just need the right conditions for it to be expressed.

The experience of the transcendent is that of the unbounded ocean of consciousness, the field of infinite creativity. Accessing this deep silence is a fundamental means for anyone to easily release his or her inner, dormant creativity. In addition, the deep rest gained during Transcendental Meditation helps to relieve the stress and anxiety that often restrict the natural flow of creativity. Some people think that stress is necessary in order to create. I don't agree with that line of thinking. The act of creativity is an extremely joyful experience; otherwise no one would ever create!!

In his book, *Catching the Big Fish*, the great filmmaker David Lynch describes the creative process:

> Here's how it works: Inside every human being is an ocean of pure, vibrant consciousness. When you "transcend" in Transcendental Meditation you dive down into that ocean of pure consciousness. You splash into it. And it's bliss. You can vibrate with this bliss. Experiencing pure consciousness enlivens it, expands it. It starts to unfold and grow... You can catch ideas at a deeper level. And creativity really flows. It makes life more like a fantastic game.[2]

The great Austrian composer Richard Strauss, famous for his waltzes, discussed how he composed:

> Composing is a procedure that is not so readily explained. When the inspiration comes, it is something of so subtle, tenuous, will-o-the-wisp-like nature that it almost defies definition. When in my most inspired moods, I have definite compelling visions, involving a higher selfhood. I feel at such moments that I am tapping the source of Infinite and Eternal energy from which you and I and all things proceed.[3]

Many artists and musicians describe this effortless experience of creativity in which they feel they are not doing anything and the process of creation is happening by itself. They become so absorbed in the process of their creation that time disappears, and even their ego dissolves. Athletes have also expressed this experience of pure wakefulness while working out or in a competition, and refer to it as being "in the zone."

The following poem called "Am I the Poet?" expresses my experience of watching the poem write itself as though I had no involvement in writing it.

Am I The Poet?

Am I the poet of this poem
of each expression rising from within?
Silence stirred, an impulse heard
beyond all meter, beyond all word . . .

Am I the writer of these lines?
Each phrase appearing on my screen
is just a seed sown for silence to flow
in any way the wind blows . . .

Am I the composer of this song
of the sounds of silence singing?
Wholeness bent, on self-intent
for me to be silence's instrument . . .

Can I claim popular authorship
when I am just a joyous witness
of each lyrical notion in the swelling ocean
of pure silence in tender motion?

Experiences

During my Transcendental Meditation Sidhi Program [see Chapter 8], my mind is deeply engaged and absorbed in the process. Then when I come out of meditation and sit to write, my mind is quiet, and I pick up the thread of the thought that is arising in my mind and write it down. Often just starting to write is enough to keep the thoughts flowing, and my hand writes in order to get down the thoughts that my mind is "dictating." When the pure consciousness is very strong, and my mind is very settled—after meditation, for example—it is such a joy for my unbounded Self to witness the thoughts arising from my mind and being written down on paper.

C.C.—Vermont

TM made me feel less anxious immediately. The more I meditated, the calmer I felt; the calmer I felt, the more organized I became; the more organized I became, the more time I had during the day. The more time I had during the day, the more productive I could be. The more productive I was, the more I could find the time to meditate—PERFECT!

C.K.—South Africa

Even though most of my family does not know that I meditate, they all can tell a big difference in my life: they've seen my blood pressure going down, my eating habits becoming better, my just all-round happiness and never stressing anymore and just going about my life as it comes. They've noticed a big change in me.

G.L.—New York

4
COSMIC CONSCIOUSNESS —
BEING IN THE ZONE

"The state of cosmic consciousness should be the state of normal human consciousness. Any state below cosmic consciousness can only be taken to be subnormal human consciousness. The human mind should be a cosmically conscious mind."[1]

— Maharishi

My brother once told me about a time when he was giving a speech at a business conference when suddenly he felt he was watching himself give the presentation. In 1974, I taught an elderly lady Transcendental Meditation. Soon after she learned, she described to me a similar experience in which, while practicing TM, she saw herself meditating, as if she were outside looking in. I have heard and read many accounts of these types of experiences from people of all walks of life. They are natural, normal occurrences, but most people do not understand the experience they are having, or have any reference or framework in which to put them.

One of Maharishi's extraordinary contributions to the understanding of consciousness is the disclosure of seven states of human consciousness. Everyone is familiar with the first three states—waking, dreaming, and sleeping. The fourth state of consciousness is transcendental consciousness, which was explained in the previous chapter as the silent, unbounded Self of everyone. The experience of transcendental consciousness is the basis of the next three states of consciousness—cosmic consciousness, God consciousness, and unity consciousness.

Cosmic consciousness, the fifth state of consciousness, is transcendental consciousness lived along with the waking, dreaming, and sleeping states of consciousness. This means that the experience of unbounded transcendental consciousness is stabilized in one's awareness even while active or during sleep.

Have you ever had the experience of knowing that you are asleep, or watching yourself sleeping? This is an experience of pure wakefulness during sleep. Anyone can have a flash of this experience now and then. Maharishi has explained that when this experience becomes a daily, or rather a nightly reality, where even the deep dullness of sleep does not overshadow the experience of inner wakefulness, it is a clear indication of stabilized transcendental consciousness. The mind remains awake inside, lit up like a softly glowing light bulb. What a nice way to experience being asleep every night!

I remember once watching Oprah Winfrey on one of her shows. I can't remember which show it was or who she was interviewing, but she said she often watched herself sleeping at night. I wanted to call up or Skype into the show right away to say: "You are experiencing the state of cosmic consciousness, the experience of inner wakefulness or witnessing during deep sleep."

Cosmic consciousness grows as the nervous system becomes freed from stress. It's like dipping a cloth into yellow dye and then putting it into the sun. In the sun, most of the dye fades away, but a little of the yellow remains. By repeatedly putting the cloth into the dye and repeatedly putting it into the sun, eventually the yellow adheres to the cloth and does not fade away. Likewise, by repeatedly experiencing transcendental consciousness and then plunging into activity, one begins to enjoy the qualities of pure consciousness—more calmness, stability, energy, and joy—throughout the day. However, by the end of the day, some of the qualities have faded away.

Over time these inner qualities remain steadier in daily life just like the yellow in the cloth. Eventually there comes a time when no amount of stress or impressions in activity can overshadow the brilliant reality of pure consciousness.

Flashes of cosmic consciousness can be compared to the experience of being "in the zone," as it is commonly called today. Many people, especially athletes, artists, and musicians, have had a glimpse of pure consciousness during activity. The experience is often expressed as witnessing one's actions, as though one is outside looking in at the situation and the activity is experienced as completely effortless and automatic, as though one is not doing anything at all. The feeling is of being in an effortless flow, or "in the zone."

The *Tao te Ching* describes this experience of being in the zone: "When once you are free from all seeming, from all craving and lusting, then will you move of your own impulse, without so much as knowing that you move."[2]

Jacques d'Amboise, the popular dancer and teacher, described moments when he felt completely in command, that he could do anything with his body: "When you are dancing like that, you seem to be removed. You can enjoy yourself doing it and watch yourself doing it at the same time."[3]

The entire Trinity College girls' squash team, which was third in the nation in 2010, learned Transcendental Meditation as a tool to improve their athletic performance. Nour Bahgat, an Egyptian member of the Trinity team, was the #1 Women's U.S. collegiate player in 2009. She says that the Transcendental Meditation technique helps her get into "the zone". "Being in the zone is very important for an athlete because that's the point where you can perform at your best level," she says.[4]

Ralph Waldo Emerson wrote in his famous essay, "Self-Reliance," "The great man is he who in the midst of the crowd keeps with perfect sweetness the independence of solitude."[5] This is a perfect description of an experience of cosmic consciousness. Even while you are acting, there is a silent, yet very sweet state of inner freedom.

This experience does not occur by trying to be silent inside or by trying to be detached in any way. Cosmic consciousness grows naturally over time through repeated experience of transcendental consciousness alternated with activity. This alternation cultures the nervous system to support the coexistence of transcendental consciousness along with waking, dreaming, and sleeping. Spontaneously enjoying this natural state of inner calmness and equanimity throughout daily life allows a person to act more wisely and effectively in any situation.

Maharishi has said that if the small individual self is not able to have its own independent status, then we are always dependent on the surrounding circumstances—we are not able to stand on our own feet. Life becomes dependent on the object and we are weak, tossed about by the changing circumstances of life. When the individual self has permanently gained its immovable, unlimited status in cosmic consciousness, then we are established in freedom. We are then able to evaluate and appreciate the outer or "objective" value of life in its completeness, on the ground of the full development of the subject, the "big Self." On this basis, the next state of consciousness, God consciousness, begins to unfold.

Here is a poem expressing the experience of witnessing, being "in the zone," or cosmic consciousness.

Letting Go

When I am feeling happy, relaxed and carefree
something magical happens—a true mystery.
Nature smiles her luck on me
fulfilling my desires effortlessly.

These pure moments of completely letting go
complications of the past—present in a flow,
slipping into automatic, like wind that blows—
non-doing—I witness life's beautiful show.

The more I succumb to inner gravity,
pulling me into purest serenity,
outer life then reflects this inner identity—
a silent charioteer, guiding me peacefully.

When I stop straining, everything comes—
a great secret we all need to learn from.
The more we sink into the golden sun,
the more effortlessly all gets done.

Experiences

When I close my eyes to take rest for the night, I find myself fully awake within. I am lit up from within and this light lights up the cosmos inside. Thousands and thousands of shimmering points glorify the depth of endless space. I move with it, yet I do not move. I feel established in inner peace and sweetest, natural, most nourishing bliss. I enjoy how the shimmering points move into mandala (circular) shapes, from the biggest to the smallest, enjoying the most spectacular and at the same time most natural display of my Self.

P.P.—Denmark

I have had the experience of feeling, or being, the huge unbounded field of consciousness—that is who I am, and I see the sequence of time in my individual life as if I am viewing it from a distance. I see time (my life) coming from the past and continuing into the future, like a train, and I see where I am now. When I come out of meditation I see myself as if stepping onto that train of activity. I am watching it, my individuality simply steps into activity and goes through the necessary motions that need to be done, but I am separate from it; the activity does not touch my essential nature, my essential Self does not become involved in it.

C.C.—Vermont

One day I had an especially sweet meditation session. Afterwards I felt the sweetness and tenderness of the environment around me. As I later retired for the night and closed my eyes, very intense self-effulgent concentrated specks of golden light in motion—and no motion at the same time—started zooming forth. This went on throughout the night—I was "awake" all night long, witnessing the zooming forth of the light. In the morning I felt very rested and exhilarated.

S.W.—Slovenia

I went straight to sleep shortly after 10 p.m. and about half an hour later I noticed an inner wakefulness and was witnessing my sleep very clearly. There was a bar of bright light in my navel area that was rippling with bliss, then a sensation of coming out very smoothly, as if from a deep well, and the thought, "that was the most amazing silence." A few nights later the bliss returned, rippling slowly upwards on the body, and going on for several hours during the night on several occasions, as well as in the daytime.

D.R.—England

5
GOD CONSCIOUSNESS

"To live a normal human life is to live a life of divine consciousness, God consciousness. A normal human mind should function on human levels and yet have the status of universal cosmic mind."[1]

— Maharishi

Just as musicians have a natural ear for sound and patterns of sound, artists have a natural vision for more refined values of form. In Holland, the country of the great Dutch masters such as Van Gogh, Rembrandt, and Vermeer, the sun does not set until 11:00 at night during summer. From about 6:00 p.m. to 11:00 p.m., the light shimmering through the trees is soft and sparkling, like a setting for a fairy tale. If you are still, observing nature, you can see the minute particles that make up the light casting its magical spell. When I lived in Holland, I remember thinking that for an artist, this would be the perfect place to paint—no wonder there are so many famous Dutch painters. I believe these master painters were able to perceive the formless particles that structure form. Perceiving the finest level of existence that makes up form is called God consciousness.

Maharishi identifies God consciousness as the sixth state of consciousness. The name God consciousness may sound quite unapproachable and of course religious, but it is important to understand that this state it is not tied to any one religion, and that many people from all cultures and backgrounds have had spontaneous experiences of God consciousness. These experiences come from around the world and span all generations. This again shows that God consciousness is natural to everyone and stems from the universal reality of existence.

You may wonder: what about people who don't believe in God? Is God consciousness dependent on belief in a supreme being or higher power? In fact, God consciousness has nothing to do with any belief; it is a higher state of consciousness that develops naturally from cosmic consciousness.

As I mentioned in the last chapter, when the non-changing level of transcendental consciousness has been permanently stabilized in cosmic consciousness, one has gained a state of freedom or, in scientific terms, a state of complete "field independence." From this state of freedom, we are in a position to fully appreciate the whole sensory range of life.

When we reach cosmic consciousness, our senses of perception have become free from stress. Through the continual process of transcending, the entire physiology is normalized and perceptions become more refined. We gain the ability to perceive finer and finer values of the world around us until we reach the subtlest level, which exists at the junction point of diversity and unity—the finest level that borders the transcendent.

Maharishi once used an analogy from the field of art to explain the growth of cosmic consciousness into God consciousness. The more we are capable of appreciating the fine details of the artwork, the more we can perceive how the finest brush strokes of the artist created the art. As this appreciation develops, we begin to see how the mind of the artist worked, how the creation of the art came about. We become familiar with the creator by intimately knowing every detail of the artwork.

Physics tells us that matter is made of particles and that particles are actually waves, or frequencies. When perception becomes more refined, we begin to perceive these finer particles and levels of existence that make up creation. Meditators report that during Transcendental Meditation finer levels of inner perception have a celestial quality; they perceive a field filled with light that dances, sparkles, and shimmers. They often observe a myriad of brilliant points of light that sometimes form into various patterns, or perceive thick, liquid waves of light and bliss.

Just as these celestial experiences exist in inner awareness, they are also noticeable on the "outer" level of perception during activity. As we appreciate finer and finer details of the surroundings, nature starts to sparkle. The objects of perception become more glorious and fulfilling. Right from their beginning days of transcending, people notice that everything around them appears brighter and clearer; they start to perceive more comprehensively and, at the same time, pick up finer details of their environment.

The French artist Georges Seurat's painting, *A Sunday on La Grande Jatte*, is one example of refined perception. This beautiful rendering of a typical Sunday scene next to the river is composed entirely of small colorful points. From a distance, you see the complete forms and do not notice the points that comprise them. Close up, you see a universe of multicolored points. In the growth from cosmic consciousness to God consciousness, our perception naturally becomes refined to appreciate not just the surface form of objects, but simultaneously to appreciate all the values that make up the form.

Experiences of refined perception can occur in many different ways, such as the perception of the more celestial, light-filled value of existence. A woman correspondent noted that while she was playing golf, "All the fairways and greens and people on the course were filled with a holy light."[2]

In this experience, the journalist recognized the golf course and at the same time saw it shining with a celestial quality of light. When we are able to perceive the surface value of an object, the finest relative value of the object, and the transcendental value of the object—all at the same time—we are experiencing the whole range of creation.

Helen Keller, who was deaf and blind from the age of two, was not able to visually perceive the outer surface value but was still able to experience the transcendental light value of pure consciousness, which she describes in her book *My Religion*:

I sense a holy passion pouring down from the springs of Infinity. . . . Bound to suns and planets by invisible cords, I feel the flame of eternity in my soul. Here, in the midst of the every-day air, I sense the rush of ethereal rains. I am conscious of the splendor that binds all things of earth to all things of heaven—immured by silence and darkness, I possess the light which shall give me vision a thousand-fold when death sets me free.[3]

Experiences of the celestial value of creation are extremely tender and intimate. These finer levels of creation are so charming and blissful that feelings of gratitude naturally start to bubble up in appreciation for these personal experiences of divine bliss. As you start to experience these finer levels of creation, the heart begins to open up and flow.

When we are directly experiencing the source of all creation, it is natural to desire a firsthand meeting with the Creator, the Divine Artist, God—or whomever or whatever you choose to call this creative intelligence. It is important to emphasize that this experience does not depend on anyone's religion, faith, or cultural background. It is natural that when something good happens to us, we feel it is a miracle of God, or an unexplained blessing, and spontaneously feel to thank God. This does not mean we are following a religion. We just naturally feel an opening of our heart—the upsurge of feelings of love, appreciation, and gratitude.

The quality of the heart flowing is love. Love is the most unifying value of life. The power of love, the light of love, allows the vision to perceive the most delicate, tender, refined, and hidden values of life. The resulting appreciation of the celestial value in everything is the development of God consciousness. Maharishi has explained that love growing in our hearts is what takes the supreme celestial value of the object to the infinite, transcendental value of Being.

The beginning stages of unity consciousness occur as this love—or swelling of the heart—starts to flow out through all the senses of perception. This flow of love bridges the feeling of separation experienced in cosmic consciousness between the unbounded, inner transcendental consciousness and the outer world. The heart becomes like a cup of liquid nectar that rises until it starts to overflow and spill into the environment, thus connecting the inner with the outer. Rather than witnessing the outside as separate from yourself, as in cosmic consciousness, you begin to enjoy seeing your own bliss, the infinite value of your own Self, reflected everywhere. This is the experience of unity consciousness dawning.

The path from transcendental consciousness to cosmic consciousness is the path of the full development of the mind, whereas the path from cosmic consciousness to God consciousness cultures the full development of the heart. The full development of both the heart and the mind is the basis for unity consciousness.

Here is a poem expressing more refined celestial perceptions in meditation, which have been growing in my life.

Shimmering

Shimmering darkness,
shimmering space,
shimmering wholeness
of each point encased
in shimmering circles
opening into waves
of spiraling particles
in my silent enclave.

Shimmering you come
in a stirring rush
awakening the hum
of the shimmering hush.
Shimmering you rain,
shimmering you flow,
filling my domain
with your glistening glow,
like thousands of suns
and the shining moon
upon the rippling ocean
of my liquid cocoon.

Shimmering darkness, simmering still
showering you ever reappear,
spreading sweetest blissful thrills
shimmering crystal clear.

Experiences

During my meditation my awareness gradually collapsed inward and I became conscious of different levels in my being. The inner levels were more deep, dense, dark and still; the outer levels were lighter, brighter, with more lively awareness. As I continued my practice the more dense, central core of my being became more filled with light. By the end of my meditation, I was becoming aware of the divine essence of all dimensions of creation.

B.G.—England

Immediately after learning Transcendental Meditation I noticed how everything in nature appeared infinitely richer in color and texture. I had never observed such beauty before. My perception of the world around me had physically transformed with the removal of deep stress and fatigue from my physiology. This appreciation of nature's beauty was, and has continued to be, such a joy!

J.B.—Australia

As a result of my practice of Transcendental Meditation and the Transcendental Meditation Sidhi Program [see Chapter 8] I am living an inner richness, which I experience as wave upon wave of gratitude. All actions as well as non-actions are stirs and non-stirs of gratitude. Gratitude pours in and pours out. It makes me see clearly and everything is known, nothing is foreign. It is like knowing the alphabet and reading the script of the universe. I see how everything is very well and wisely put, how everything is exactly as it should be, and the plan is magnificent.

P.P.—Denmark

My practice of the Transcendental Meditation Sidhi Program brings increasingly tender and delicate feelings, which pierce deep into my heart and stir waves of devotion. This devotion pours forth to the Divine, and the Divine seems to pour forth love and blessings back to me. Some of these blessings are intangible, spiritual blessings that are exquisite or glorious or illuminating beyond anything I ever knew existed. It is a humbling and inexpressibly melting experience, which I cherish as Divine Grace.

H.S.—Canada

6
UNITY CONSCIOUSNESS

*"In unity consciousness, what prevails is the infinite value of life.
Perception of the relative dances, sings, rejoices, and glorifies itself in the value
of the infinite."*[1]

— Maharishi

Every Easter Sunday in my hometown in Florida, there is a sunrise service on the beach. I remember once on the eve of that special service, when I was about sixteen years old, I could not sleep all night in anticipation. At about 5:30 a.m., I went around the house waking everybody up, hoping someone would go with me. I managed to get a couple of family members together and off we went down the beach to the service. I sensed something extremely magical that morning. I felt I was in love with everyone I saw, even strangers, and I also felt in love with the entirety of the environment—the calm aqua ocean, the palm trees gently swaying in the wind, the warm balmy breeze upon my face. My heart was wide open, and I could physically feel love flow from my heart, gently embracing everyone and everything. This flow connected me with my surroundings, and I felt one with all creation. I realize now it was a glimpse of unity consciousness.

In unity consciousness, we experience the infinite, absolute level of life—pure consciousness itself—in everything. It is the same pure consciousness we experience deep within ourselves in the state of transcendental consciousness. It is our own Self, and mysteriously, it is also the Self of the whole universe. This is what is often referred to as "oneness," because a profound connection is experienced between the inner and outer.

The foreword to Maharishi's book *Science of Being and Art of Living* states:

In Unity Consciousness every particle of creation, even the farthest, most distant point of the universe, is experienced as a wave in the unbounded ocean of Transcendental Consciousness, which is one's own Self. Everything in the universe—even at the very ends of the universe—is found to be the reverberations of my own Self, of my own unbounded consciousness.[2]

Through every faculty of perception—sight, hearing, touch, taste, smell—the experience of the Self dominates—the experience of unity, harmony, wholeness, and fullness. We experience the entire world as our own projection—as waves in the ocean of our unbounded consciousness, as waves of the Self. We see the infinite value of the Self in every perception. We also still perceive the differences, but unity predominates in our awareness. The boundaries of perception no longer overshadow the essential nature of life. This is realization of the ultimate reality—enlightenment. Maharishi describes this state in his commentary on the Bhagavad-Gita:

The height of realization ... is to realize the supreme oneness of life in terms of one's own Self. No diversity of life is able to detract from this state of supreme Unity. One who has reached It is the supporter of all and everything, for he is life eternal. He bridges the gulf between the relative and the Absolute....Yoga [Union] in this state has reached its perfection; there is no level of Union higher than this that he has gained. He stands established on the ultimate level of consciousness.[3]

I enjoyed another experience of unity several years after I learned Transcendental Meditation. During a tennis match, my opponent hit me a high lob shot. Suddenly time seemed to dissolve into super slow motion. I was in a vast sea in which everything and everyone was part of a timeless, thick consciousness. My awareness was so expanded that I had difficulty locating the tennis ball in the air, although I ended up hitting a perfect shot without any feeling of doing. An upsurge of joy filled my being to the point where the whole situation seemed comical, almost absurd—putting my attention on hitting a tiny tennis ball in the midst of this immense vast reality of consciousness! The whole experience lasted maybe 30 seconds, but the memory of it has remained my entire life.

The great scientist Albert Einstein eloquently described such an experience of unity consciousness:

> There are moments when one feels free from one's own identification with human limitations and inadequacies. At such moments one imagines that one stands on some spot of a small planet gazing in amazement at the cold yet profoundly moving beauty of the eternal, the unfathomable. Life and death flow into one and there is neither evolution nor destiny, only Being.[4]

An excerpt from "The Over-Soul" by Ralph Waldo Emerson, an essay first published in 1841, also expresses the reality of unity consciousness:

> ...within man is the soul of the whole; the wise silence; the universal beauty, to which every part and particle is equally related; the eternal ONE. And this deep power in which we exist and whose beatitude is all accessible to us, is not only self-sufficing and perfect in every hour, but the act of seeing and the thing seen, the seer and the spectacle, the subject and the object, are one. We see the world piece by piece, as the sun, the moon, the animal, the tree; but the whole, of which these are the shining parts, is the soul.[5]

The actor William Shatner, who became famous for his role as Captain Kirk in the popular television show *Star Trek*, is also an equestrian and describes an experience he has had that gives a flavor of unity both while acting and horseback riding:

> As an actor, first of all to have that feeling of oneness with whatever it is you are doing, you have to be good enough at it to dispense with the techniques. If you are a skier you are skiing the hill, you are not wondering if I can stay upright. On a horse, you've long since forgotten where your feet should be. It all becomes part of the unity of what you're doing, and I have felt innumerable times a unity with the horse I am riding, so that the horse and I are one. The horse is running and it's me running. There is communication between [me and] the horse. The horse is in my lap, and I am in the horse's head. It's all one thing.

And that same thing applies to being an actor on the stage where the audience somehow mystically, the audience lines of communication enter my head and leave me and become part of the audience. So there is a unity of actor and audience that I have felt many times. I know when I reach it. It's like an athlete being on the pipes—you're running and its effortless.[6]

I wrote the following poem to express the growth of consciousness from transcendental consciousness to unity consciousness.

Fourth through Seventh States of Consciousness

Transcendental Consciousness
As I step into my fourth dimension,
all perception melts before me.
Like the canvas of an abstract painting
all forms and colors are fading
into a soft, silent sea.

Cosmic Consciousness
Stepping into my fifth dimension,
I feel outside looking in
to the ever-changing times
of the world that seems out of rhyme
with my silence that flows within.

God Consciousness
Stepping into my sixth dimension,
life takes on a transparent glow.
A divine texture glorifies my sight,
dancing like golden sunlight
sparkling on freshly fallen snow.

Unity Consciousness
Stepping into my seventh dimension,
my silence penetrates through life's layers,
through my senses in all directions.
Everything is my Self's inner perfection,
singing Self's beauty everywhere.

Experiences

The fulfilling experience of Unity Consciousness has been gradually and completely naturally becoming the dominant reality of my daily life. It is most fulfilling because in this experience I truly feel oneness with each wonderful person I meet, the near and far environment, and with almost any situation. Everyone and everything reflects the bliss of my own Being. Unity first started in occasional, isolated moments many years ago, a few months after learning the Transcendental Meditation technique. Over the years, waves of wholeness have steadily increased. Now, my life feels flooded with an ocean of consciousness, inner and outer. The growth has been so effortless that I rarely think about it.

S.K.—Pennsylvania

During a group practice of Transcendental Meditation one day, I opened my eyes feeling overwhelmed with bliss and peace. I looked around and everyone and everything was glowing with bliss and happiness. I realized that everyone and everything and myself are one with the ultimate reality of life.

M.T.F.—Philippines

Recently our washing machine broke and I had to go to a laundromat. Thinking that it would be an unpleasant experience, I was surprised when I walked in and felt bliss at the sight of clothes tumbling in the machines. It triggered the feeling I have in meditation of my awareness spiraling inward, as it curls upon itself, tumbling endlessly in bliss. This feeling of bliss continued with me as I loaded the clean clothes into the car and started down the road for home. My inner bliss began spreading out to the headlights of approaching cars and then to the lighted windows of the homes I passed. It seemed to touch every star in the sky. I felt oneness with the universe and that the universe was returning bliss to me. The back and forth of our relationship created a fabric of light that was just myself knowing itself. Everything was perfect, timeless, and divine.

J.B.—North Carolina

7
KINGDOM OF HEAVEN WITHIN

"Having the Kingdom of Heaven within you, you have no right to suffer in life; you have only to enjoy the grace of God."[1]

— Maharishi

My life took another unusual turn after meditating for about a year. Spontaneously, I started to become fascinated with religious scriptures.

My mother was Episcopalian and my father was Catholic. When they married, my mother had to promise the Catholic Church she would raise her children as Catholics. As a result of that dictum, my mother said the first prejudice she ever had was against Catholics. She told my father that if he wanted to raise us as Catholics, go right ahead!

My father had a strong Catholic background. His father and mother were extremely devoted to the Catholic Church. My grandfather received the Knight of Saint Gregory award from the Pope as a result of his dedication and generosity to the church. My father was one of the most genuine people I have ever known. I also feel he was a deeply spiritual person and a sincere seeker. He saw a lot of hypocrisy in the church and, I think because of that, one day right before he was about to go on a flying mission in World War II, he told his priest that he wanted to be ex-communicated from the church. The priest told him he would die and go to hell!

Consequently, I did not have much of a strong religious upbringing. We went to church on Christmas and Easter and that was about it. When I was about 17 years old, my brother, then at the University of North Carolina, became involved in a Christian community. I went and visited him once. I prayed with his friends. Several of them talked to me about asking Christ into my life, which I did. I never felt any change or any inspiration from this endeavor. At times I felt a bit turned off when his friends would try to push their religious beliefs on me. The words in the Bible just did not have any direct meaning for me, although I found some of Christ's sayings extremely uplifting.

I traveled a lot and sometimes I would read the Bible in a hotel room. After I had been meditating for a while, certain phrases in the Bible, which I had heard now and then throughout my life, such as "The Kingdom of Heaven is within you" (Luke 17:21) and "Be still, and know that I am God" (Psalm 46:10) started to have direct meaning. I felt I was beginning to experience the "Kingdom of Heaven within," and that experience continues to become more real and meaningful as time goes on.

My experience of stillness, or transcendental consciousness, has become vast and universal, often blazing with intensely brilliant, even blinding, light. Words cannot even begin to describe the intensity of bliss and the tenderness of emotions that not only swell in my heart, but penetrate into every pore of my being. Is this an experience of God? I don't know if it is God for sure, but I can definitely say without a doubt it is the "Kingdom of Heaven within".

Again, it is important to emphasize that this experience is not based on any particular religious belief but is a purely spiritual experience that anyone can enjoy, no matter what their religious background, beliefs, or lack thereof.

This poem describes my growing experiences of heaven within.

Kingdom of Heaven

I desire your Grace.
You come to me,
as rivers race
into a motionless sea,
as luminous beams
of waltzing light
that close the seams
of the dark night.
I knock on your door
and turn the key,
I enter your core
of silent luxury—
a gilded vestibule
of mandalic symmetry
encrusted with jewels
affording felicity,
a palatial home
of regal splendor
a sacred dome
of self-surrender.
I climb the stairs
that spiral
into the glare
of mirrored aisles,
that Self-reflect
Self's vision
and re-project
Self's cognition.
I open the window
to sky's ornament—
a soft rainbow
of Heaven's descent.
Touching both ends
of the universe,
infinity bends
Heaven to earth.
I call your Grace—
you sweetly come.
In your embrace
is Heaven's kingdom.
The royal decree
your whisper imparts,
to love God eternally
with all my heart.

Experiences

One day during my Transcendental Meditation my head became full of light and the room was full of sunlight (and yet it was totally cloudy outside). It was beautiful. I felt healed, safe and full of nature's forgiveness. After meditation I lay down for a few minutes and I felt as if I was lying gently in heaven's cradle.

J.C.—England

Sometimes in meditation I experience deep silence, being in an unbounded empty space. Sometimes I see light in that empty space like the sun.

U—Mongolia

Sometimes during meditation golden light pours into my head, as if squeezed through a cloth, filling my head with light. At times, I feel like a newborn baby entering a new dimension of reality made of infinite tenderness, purity, love, and divine wholeness, a heavenly domain.

B.B.—England

As soon as I close my eyes and start TM there is an all-pervading softness and peace. Thoughts subside as the waves of the ocean settle and become still. I am left in bliss-filled silence. What thoughts may come do not break the surface of the ocean; I remain in a heavenly state of complete stillness and bliss. When I open the eyes after meditation the world is new, I remain an ocean of bliss and light and silence as I move through my dynamic day. I am so sublimely peaceful and blissful while walking the paths of my life on earth, which themselves merge into that unbounded silence.

K.D.—Vermont

During my Transcendental Meditation Sidhi Program [see chapter 8] I experienced a Milky Way spiraling slowly in the field of consciousness. I feel as if I am just floating in a translucent field of bliss. The silence is very deep and soothing. It feels like being cradled in the divine wholeness of life. Sometimes there is a sweet pressure of bliss in the heart and the heart is so full of bliss, the feeling is: I am in heaven.

B.B.—England

8
TRANSCENDENTAL MEDITATION SIDHI PROGRAM

"Every hop becomes a cosmic smile for the whole creation."[1]

—Maharishi

I had been meditating for four years when, in 1976, Maharishi introduced an advanced technology of consciousness—the Transcendental Meditation Sidhi Program—to accelerate the growth of higher states of consciousness. I already felt like I was on a jet plane of evolution, but now I was about to board a rocket ship!

The word *sidhi* means perfection, and the *sidhi sutras*, or aphorisms, are contained in the Yoga Sutras of Maharishi Patanjali, an aspect of the ancient Vedic literature.[2] The second sutra of the Yoga Sutras says *Yogash chitta vritti nirodhah*: "Yoga is the complete settling of the activity of the mind."

Through Transcendental Meditation, you experience the deepest silence of your Self—transcendental consciousness. The Transcendental Meditation Sidhi Program (TM-Sidhi® program), which includes the Yogic Flying® technique, develops the ability of the individual to spontaneously think and act from this most subtle and powerful level of awareness. Functioning from the level of transcendental consciousness naturally results in more expansive, creative thinking and greater success in effortlessly achieving one's goals.

In addition, the Transcendental Meditation Sidhi Program helps to develop and refine the full potential of one's mind, heart, and body. Maharishi often described this development using the analogy of a house. You have a big house but are accustomed to using only two or three rooms in the house such as the kitchen, bedroom, and living room. If you become acquainted with all the rooms in the house, you naturally begin to make use of them in daily life. Like that, after practicing the Transcendental Meditation Sidhi Program, you become acquainted with the totality of pure consciousness and begin to use more and more of the full potential of the mind in daily life.

Maharishi has explained that anything is possible from the field of pure consciousness because it is the home of all the laws of nature, the source of all creation. The Transcendental Meditation Sidhi Program trains the mind to function from this deepest, most powerful level. As a result, desires are fulfilled more and more automatically.

I am sure you are wondering at this point about Yogic Flying! Do you really levitate? How is it even possible? First of all, at this point in time, no one practicing the Yogic Flying technique is reporting floating or flying through the air. But there are over 100,000 people around the world who are enjoying the first stages of yogic flying, which looks like hopping. Hopping! This probably sounds strange, even ridiculous. It's important to understand that it is not the outer phenomenon—the actual hopping—that is important, but rather the inner bubbling bliss, the total brain functioning that develops with regular practice, and the stabilization of pure consciousness experienced by Yogic Flyers.

When practicing the Yogic Flying technique, a person sits cross-legged, or in the lotus position if comfortable, although this is not a prerequisite to practicing it. People of all ages, shapes, and sizes have learned Yogic Flying. Critics say that anyone can sit cross-legged and bounce across a room. However, on one occasion, some professional gymnasts tried to imitate the Yogic Flying practice. Although some of the athletes were able to hop across the room seated in lotus, it was only with a lot of effort and exertion and for a very short time. In contrast, people who practice Yogic Flying report experiences of complete effortlessness. They experience a faint impulse of energy deep in their silence. The next thing they know they are hopping across the room with very little awareness of the body as the mind is drawn inward, enjoying the experience of transcendence at the same time. After the session, they feel energized and refreshed.

I was fortunate to attend one of the first courses at which Yogic Flying was taught. Several hotels on Lake Lucerne, Switzerland, had been rented during the off-season to house many course participants—around 500 at that time. It was such an exciting, intriguing time to be learning something that was so unusual and truly thrilling. Maharishi was connected by phone to all the courses every day, and every time course participants lifted off the ground for the first time, they would report their experiences to him.

Course participants commonly described that when they lifted off, they had very little awareness of their body, their consciousness felt extremely expanded, and they felt a rising and swelling up of bliss inside. Afterwards in activity, they reported feeling lightness in their body and, as the expansion of awareness continued, they sometimes felt they wanted to just laugh and laugh. Those of us on the course felt that this was a precious and historic time of cosmic proportions.

Among countless examples, one course participant gave the following experience of her first time lifting off, or hopping:

> I was very deep in silence. I started to feel my body gently rock, then I felt this upsurge of energy flow through me, and the next thing I knew I was sitting on the other end of the room. I had very little awareness of my body moving across the room. My whole being felt exhilarated, and I just wanted to laugh aloud.

Objectively, the exhilarating and blissful experience of Yogic Flying shows an exceptionally high level of coherence (orderliness) in brain functioning, peaking at the point of lift-off.[3] Scientific research shows that higher levels of brainwave coherence, as indicated by EEG (electroencephalography) measurements, are associated with greater creativity and neurological efficiency, greater conceptual ability, and higher levels of principled moral reasoning.[4]

There is another wonderful side benefit of the Yogic Flying technique. In the early 1960s, Maharishi predicted that when one percent of any given population practiced Transcendental Meditation, there would be an upsurge of positivity and a decrease of negative trends in the surrounding environment. This effect was scientifically verified and named the Maharishi Effect in honor of Maharishi.[5] In 1976, when he introduced the Transcendental Meditation Sidhi Program, Maharishi predicted that because it is a more powerful technology for enlivening the field of pure consciousness at the basis of all existence, a significantly smaller number—the square root of one percent of a population—practicing together in groups should be sufficient to produce measurable positive effects in society. This effect is called the "Extended Maharishi Effect" or the "Super Radiance Effect".

Nearly 50 research studies,[6] many of which have been published in leading scientific journals, including a study published in the *Journal of Conflict Resolution*,[7] verify this phenomenon of the Maharishi Effect.

These studies show that a measurable influence of coherence and harmony is generated in society by the group, resulting in decreased negative trends, including reduced crime, accidents, civil conflicts and violence; and increased positive trends, including rising economic indicators and improved overall quality of life.

When students and teachers of schools and universities participate in the group practice of Yogic Flying, they accelerate the development of their full creative potential, and at the same time they create a powerful influence of positivity in their community and—if the group is large enough—for the whole society and even the nation.

An increasing number of schools have implemented Transcendental Meditation and sometimes also the Transcendental Meditation Sidhi Program as part of the school day. The atmosphere in these schools is being transformed from stress-ridden to a haven of harmony, and the students are blossoming into the fullness of who they are meant to be—bright, happy, focused, and progressing towards fulfilling their dreams.

The experience of flying is not a new phenomenon. There are records from many religious traditions of saints actually flying. Milarepa, the national saint of Tibet, was known for having the ability to fly. One of his students wrote of him that "having obtained transcendental knowledge," he was able to demonstrate mastery of the "spiritual nature of the mind" by "flying through the sky, by walking, resting, and sleeping [upheld by levitation] in the air."[8]

St. Joseph of Copertino was known as the "flying friar" and was famous for his prolonged suspensions in the air and his high flights, often reaching the ceilings of cathedrals and the tops of trees. He was not allowed to say Mass, to take part in processions, or even to share meals in the community, because at any of these occasions he would disrupt the proceedings by rising into the air, remaining suspended for a long time.[9] There are also accounts of saints flying in India, the Middle East, and in the Native American community in the late 1800s.[10]

Maharishi has explained that floating is a natural ability of the human nervous system. The body is only held down by stresses and strain. When the body is free from stress, free of obstacles to the flow of inner intelligence, free of obstruction to the perfect coordination between mind and body, then the body can do anything the mind desires. Consciousness is a field of all possibilities. This is because it is the origin of all the laws of nature that conduct the activity of the universe. Consciousness is more basic than matter; therefore when functioning from the level of pure consciousness, we can do anything, even successfully command the body to lift in the air.

I wrote a song called "Moving in the Unmoving," which expresses this experience of moving in the deepest level of awareness as a result of the practice of the Transcendental Meditation Sidhi Program.

Moving in the Unmoving

Moving in the unmoving, calm, vast sea
Moving in the unmoving infinity
Moving in silence within me
Moving in the sea of totality

Moving in the depths of the universe
Moving in the sparkles of Heaven on Earth
Moving in silence within me
Moving in the sea of totality

Our joy is in moving the unmanifest
In pure dynamism we are at rest
Stirring the move of wholeness
Stirring the ocean to flow in fullness

Moving in the unmoving, calm, vast sea
Moving in the unmoving infinity
Moving in silence within me
Moving in the sea of totality

Experiences

During Yogic Flying I could not believe how effortlessly my body passed through the air. With only the slightest impulse I seemed to end up at the other side of the foam with this total weightless feeling at the peak of each hop. This is the closest thing to flying I have ever experienced. After some time of pure enjoyment I lay down to rest for a while only to find that same expanded, blissful awareness that had been my experience during the TM-Sidhi program; only this time every sound I perceived just added to the bliss, be it a car, a motorbike, a snore, a bird—everything was being experienced as bliss. It was like I was bathing in it; I did not want to move.

J.P.—England

During Yogic Flying my body felt hollow, porous, transparent. The awareness would expand outwards to infinity in all directions simultaneously. There were powerful surges of energy propelling the body upwards into the air. Then when my body would come down, my awareness was absorbed in deep silence, a silence sometimes washed with golden light. There was the feeling of floating in the air like a helium balloon, and later the feeling was like an astronaut floating weightlessly in outer space. Sometimes I felt like I was floating in outer space with the cosmic bodies; sometimes like a leaf blown up by the wind.

B.B.—England

The other day during Yogic Flying, I felt particularly deep and drawn into a dark, vast inner space. Within this space I saw a spiral of light slowly turning. My awareness went to the smallest, farthest point of the spiral. At that point I felt a huge upsurge of energy in my body and started to hop across the room. However, I was still so drawn into this beautiful light spiraling within that I hardly noticed I was hopping. Then I noticed a bursting of thousands of points that sparkled in the vast field of my consciousness. Time did not exist, at least for a while.

R.T.—Florida

9

ENLIGHTENMENT – IS IT POSSIBLE?

"What is important is the alternation of the Transcendental Meditation technique with daily activity. Rest and activity – this is the way to grow to enlightenment – to live life free from suffering, to live life in bliss consciousness."[1]

—Maharishi

I started meditating solely out of curiosity and the desire to turn my life in a more positive direction. I had no concept of enlightenment, nor did I seek it in any way, as the idea was so far beyond my frame of reference at the time. Enlightenment was never a topic of conversation in any religious discussions I had ever had. It was never promoted as a possibility in any church service I had attended, and it certainly was never part of my educational experience. Even without any concept of enlightenment, when I learned Transcendental Meditation I knew from the first day I started meditating that something extremely positive, profound, and transformational was taking place.

Enlightenment has long been regarded as a state reserved for a few rare individuals, a state that can only be gained by living a recluse life in a cave or in a monastery somewhere. It has been thought that enlightenment is very difficult to achieve, requiring one to give up all worldly possessions and to lead an austere life. When he started teaching throughout India and around the world, Maharishi proclaimed that enlightenment is, in fact, the most normal, natural state of life.

What is enlightenment? Enlightenment means living fullness of life, enjoying happiness or bliss 24 hours a day, every day. It means enjoying 200 percent of life—100 percent of the inner spiritual content of life along with 100 percent of the outer material value of life. It also means gaining the full support of natural law, which allows you to effortlessly fulfill your desires.

Enlightenment begins even with the first experiences of transcendental consciousness. Regular experiences of transcendental consciousness during the Transcendental Meditation technique grow spontaneously into experiences of cosmic consciousness. As stresses dissolve more and more, purity grows in the nervous system, leading to refinement of perception—experiences of God consciousness. The final stroke of enlightenment is unity consciousness, in which you feel a connection and oneness with everyone and everything in the universe. In unity consciousness you enjoy the infinite, universal value of your own Self in every object of perception and feel spiritually fulfilled, enjoying the totality of life.

"Know thyself," the inscription at the ancient temple of the Oracle of Delphi in Greece,[2] has been the advice given by the wise to people throughout the ages. As Shakespeare famously stated in *Hamlet,* "to thine own self be true." A verse in the *Tao te Ching* says:

> He who knows others is wise.
> He who knows himself is enlightened.[3]

"Know thyself" does not mean only knowing the superficial level of your own personality—the small self. It means knowing the transcendental, universal value of your "big" Self. It is important to remember that knowing yourself is not an intellectual endeavor but mainly an experiential reality. Maharishi was fond of the expression "knowing by Being". You know yourself fully by becoming that universal, unbounded value of the transcendent. As Mundaka Upanishad (1.1.3) says, "Know that by knowing which nothing else remains to be known."

Enlightenment may still sound very far-fetched, idealistic, and fanciful, but there are millions of meditators around the world who have been regularly practicing Transcendental Meditation and are enjoying concrete experiences of higher states of consciousness. They also experience more support of nature and that life flows more effortlessly.

Everyone is born with different aptitudes and tendencies in life. Some people have more intellectual capacities, others have more artistic and musical tendencies, and some have more athletic abilities. Some people have more developed qualities of the heart, some people are naturally calmer, some are more driven, etc. But, whatever our different tendencies, it is often said that most people currently use only 10–20 percent of their mental potential.

An extensive amount of scientific research on Transcendental Meditation shows increased development of brain potential.[4] After beginning the practice of Transcendental Meditation, people often notice that the natural abilities they are born with develop further, negative tendencies begin to decrease, and the stress that restricts their creativity starts to dissolve. This dissolution of stress frees more and more of the latent reserves of their brain potential.

One reason why we have so many problems in society is because the average person uses only a fraction of his or her mental potential. Partially developed minds can only create partially developed solutions. To solve the urgent problems of global proportions that the world faces today, we need to create fully developed, enlightened individuals who have an expanded vision and are able to see, with both insight and foresight, the interconnectedness of life.

When we think of what our children are exposed to at a young age on television, in the movies, in the news, and in the environment, it is really frightening. The fact that children and teenagers have confusion, dysfunction, and fear in their lives is completely predictable; they have no way to find relief from the negativity that bombards them.

Today, in most cases, schools are not unfolding greater possibilities for their students; most offer an environment of stress and pressure, which cramps creativity and restricts the blossoming of children's innate human potential. This stress may lead to a life of emotional struggles, behavioral problems, and addictions such as alcohol and drug abuse.

If we can teach our children Transcendental Meditation starting at age ten, they will have a simple tool to neutralize stress in their lives. This is so important, especially during the delicate teenage years. Teenage years should be a time when students enjoy discovering their talents and interests. The pursuit of knowledge should be a fascinating, enjoyable experience. Middle and high school is the most important time for students to establish a firm foundation for the rest of their lives. As educators, we should be giving our students the means to develop their full creative potential and, in this day and age, a technique where they can be relieved from the onslaught of the negativity and stress they are having to cope with on a daily basis.

Education should have as its goal not only high academic achievement, but also the creation of happy, well-rounded individuals who will not create problems for themselves or society. With regular practice of Transcendental Meditation, children grow up to be happy, fulfilled, enlightened adults, able to achieve their desires and contribute meaningfully to the well-being of society.

"Education for Enlightenment" should be the new paradigm and goal of education. The techniques to develop the full creative potential of every student from a young age are the most profound gifts Maharishi has given to the world. They are also the most practical means to tackle the issues prevalent everywhere today that leaders on all levels of society are desperately struggling to solve.

Maharishi once said that enlightenment is the birthright of everyone and that three basic things accelerate the growth of enlightenment:

- First and foremost, be regular in the practice of Transcendental Meditation and the Transcendental Meditation Sidhi Program.
- Maintain a regular, balanced daily routine with proper rest at night.
- Eat wholesome, pure organic foods and drink pure water.

It is important to take care of the body for overall health and well-being, which also facilitates clearer experiences of the growth of enlightenment. Maharishi points out that the path to enlightenment is a pathless path because there is nowhere to go. We simply experience the quiet level of our Self that is already there. It is just a matter of opening our awareness and experiencing that silent level. Enlightenment means being stabilized in the light of your transcendental, unbounded, blissful Self in daily life. It is the natural, all-time state of Being of everyone; we just need to wake up to it.

Another point Maharishi emphasized is that enlightenment is not something to wait for in the future—you should enjoy the unfoldment of it every day. To answer the question in the title of this chapter, "Enlightenment—Is It Possible?" Yes, enlightenment not only is possible; it is the birthright of everyone born on this earth!

Enlightenment is not a mood; it is the most real and fulfilling experience, and has objectively verifiable physical correlates, which will be explored in the next chapter. Enlightenment is the reality of living heaven in all inner and outer aspects of life. I wrote this poem based on my growing experiences of fulfillment in life, as a result of my practice of Transcendental Meditation.

Heaven

Heaven I see dancing before my eyes,
vibrant in every particle of creation;
Heaven is my silence cognized,
spurred into tenderest fluctuation.
Heaven I see alive in every flower,
the soft sky, the trees swaying in the wind;
Heaven is my Self empowered,
folding deeper and deeper within.
Heaven I see descending in waterfalls,
bubbling brooks, shimmering on the streams;
Heaven is my Self divinely enthralled,
interlaced in a thousand luminous beams.
Heaven I see glittering in the twilight,
smiling on the moon, pulsating in stars;
Heaven is my brilliant white light,
lighting the universe, near and far.
Heaven I see in dusty pastel sunsets,
angel-hair clouds, and the dawning day.
Heaven is my Self casting its net,
enveloping all in luminescent rays.
Heaven I see aglow on mountain-touched skies,
sweeping into grassy valleys below.
Heaven is my inner wakeful paradise,
in perception reflected as bliss superimposed.

Experiences

I experience silence as simple, sweet, unifying and very sublime divineness flowing. At the moment it is non-moving, unbounded stillness, non-changing, it is simultaneously fullness of perpetual change. At every moment of time flowing as silence, my Being enjoys being one with all and perceives the perfection and balance existing and permeating through all of creation.

A.W.—North Carolina

During Transcendental Meditation I became aware of a small point of light that got gradually brighter and brighter until it became blindingly white and it permeated everything. It was brighter than the sun, whiter than white, but I was able to look into it (unlike into the sun) and bathe in this perfection.

M.J.—England

I now find that the dynamic silence of my own consciousness forms a very solid mass of stability within my awareness. So massive that I find myself grounded in a BIG way within myself.

K.S.—New Hampshire

I always feel silence even after meditation. I am self-sufficient and my feelings have become more fine. Now I feel just calm…

B.S.—Mongolia

10
NEUROPHYSIOLOGY
OF ENLIGHTENMENT

*"Personal development is no longer a fantasy or only a metaphysical reality,
but it can be seen in measurable terms – physiologically, psychologically, and
sociologically."*[1]

—Maharishi

Have you ever noticed when watching a scary movie on TV that your heart starts to pound, your nerves are on edge? If a friend unexpectedly walks into the room at that moment, you may even jump or scream since you are so immersed in that emotion of fear. On the other hand, if you are watching a happy movie, you can be sitting there, so content and relaxed, that you may hardly notice if your friend walks in, since you are so absorbed in the joy from the movie.

Experiences come into our physical system through the five channels of perception—hearing, touch, sight, taste, and smell—influencing all aspects of our existence: body, mind, and emotions.

Every experience we have in life affects our brain. Seventy percent of our neuronal connections change every day based on our experience. The brain is dynamically changing, not static as previously believed. Because the mind and body are so intimately interconnected, when the mind is in a particular state, there is a corresponding influence on physiological function. If we are happy, our body creates endorphins—"happy" chemicals in our brain. If we are sad, chemicals are generated in our brain that are associated with stress and depression, and also suppress our immune system.

Simply put, every state of consciousness has its corresponding physiological state. A scientist knows if we are in the sleeping, dreaming, or waking state of consciousness just by observing our EEG (electroencephalogram—measurement of brainwaves or electrical activity). Likewise, when we transcend during the practice of the

Transcendental Meditation technique, there are specific identifiable changes that occur in neural functioning.

When I first began the practice of the Transcendental Meditation technique, I remember noticing that my breath became extremely soft and quiet. I could feel my whole body settling down. When I eventually saw the research on Transcendental Meditation, it was fascinating to see objectively what I was subjectively experiencing. It was also reassuring to know that positive, concrete, neurophysiologic changes were taking place.

Right from the beginning days of starting to teach Transcendental Meditation, Maharishi encouraged scientific research on its effects. The first research was published in March 1970 in the journal *Science*, in an article by Dr. Robert Keith Wallace entitled "Physiological Effects of the Transcendental Meditation Technique." The results of this study showed that Transcendental Meditation produces a profound state of deep rest, as seen by greatly reduced oxygen consumption, significant decreases in breathing and heart rate, deep relaxation, normalization of blood pressure, and a state of restful alertness as measured by EEG changes in the alpha and theta wave activity.[2]

Neurophysiologists have correlated several ranges of brainwave frequencies with specific states of consciousness:

- *Gamma* waves are the highest frequency waves (30Hz–100Hz) and are associated with highly focused activity and sensory perception, as well as cognitive function.
- *Beta* waves (13Hz–30Hz) indicate a state in which the brain is alert and focused on something.
- *Alpha* waves are medium frequency waves (8Hz–13Hz) that indicate a state where the brain is alert, but relaxed.
- *Theta* waves are lower frequency waves (4Hz–8Hz) that indicate a state of drowsiness such as the first stages of sleep.
- *Delta* waves are the lowest frequency waves (0.5Hz–4Hz) that indicate a state of deep sleep.

In the initial study by Dr. Wallace, the increased presence of alpha waves during Transcendental Meditation revealed that it produces a unique state of restful alertness, indicative of a fourth major state of consciousness that is physiologically and biochemically unique. Subsequent studies published soon after this first research paper further supported the original finding.[3]

In the famous poem, "Tintern Abbey," the great English poet William Wordsworth describes physiological changes that he noticed during what seems to be a vivid experience of transcendence:

...that serene and blessed mood,
in which the affections gently lead us on—
Until, the breath of this corporeal frame
And even the motion of our human blood
Almost suspended, we are laid asleep
In body, and become a living soul;
While with an eye made quiet by the power
Of harmony, and the deep power of joy,
We see into the life of things.[4]

In this experience, Wordsworth noticed that his breath and even the flow of his blood were stilled. After years of trying to recapture that state, he became frustrated and began to doubt its validity. We are so fortunate today to have a technique to daily and systematically contact this scientifically verifiable blissful state of restful alertness. Maharishi has said:

When the mind transcends during transcendental meditation, the metabolism reaches its lowest point; so does the process of breathing, and the nervous system gains a state of restful alertness which, on the physical level, corresponds to the state of bliss-consciousness, or transcendent Being.[5]

The original studies on Transcendental Meditation, which zeroed in scientifically on a fourth major state of consciousness, led to an explosion of research around the world. It would take an entire book to adequately summarize the research conducted on Transcendental Meditation. To date, over 300 peer-reviewed studies have been completed at 120 research institutes in 30 countries around the world, and have been published in many top scientific and medical journals.[6]

Dr. Norman Rosenthal, an internationally prominent psychiatrist and medical researcher, known for discovering Seasonal Affective Disorder (SAD), recently commented on the substantial body of peer-reviewed scientific studies already conducted on the Transcendental Meditation technique, in particular in the area of cardiovascular disease. Dr. Rosenthal stated that if the benefits of the TM program for heart health were contained in a pill, "It would be a billion-dollar blockbuster."[7]

One of my relatives once challenged me about the research on Transcendental Meditation by saying, "I can find research showing positive benefits for any self-development program." I countered, "Can you find any self-development program that has had over 300 scientific studies conducted in over 120 independent research institutions, documenting positive benefits physiologically, psychologically, sociologically, and even environmentally?" He did not have an answer to that statement.

This chapter highlights just a few studies that indicate growth towards the full development of consciousness. If you would like to look more deeply into the scientific research on Transcendental Meditation, please see the "For More Information" section at the back of this book.

Enlightenment unfolds through a continual process of refinement of the nervous system. As stresses are released, one begins to experience cosmic consciousness—a state in which pure consciousness exists along with the other three states of consciousness—waking, dreaming, and sleeping—as discussed in chapter 4. Even when a person in cosmic consciousness is deeply asleep, he experiences an inner alertness that Maharishi referred to as "witnessing sleep."

I remember when Maharishi used to visit courses that were regularly held in the 1970s in picturesque alpine villages of Switzerland. He would often ask the course participants whether anyone noticed that they were witnessing their sleep. Usually about half the course participants would raise their hands. Maharishi explained that the experience of the inner wakefulness of transcendental consciousness during the deep inertia of sleep is a strong indication that cosmic consciousness is becoming more stabilized.

One interesting area of research on Transcendental Meditation compares long-term and short-term meditators. A study published in 1991 in the journal *Psychophysiology* compared one-year meditators to those who had been meditating an average of nine years. The results showed that during meditation, the EEG brain wave patterns of both groups were the same, demonstrating similarly high levels of coherence.

However, outside of meditation there was a striking difference. The group that had been meditating longer showed during activity levels of coherence—orderliness of brain functioning—approaching those seen during meditation. The coherent brain functioning enlivened by transcending was becoming increasingly stabilized, available more throughout the day.[8]

In a follow-up study published in 2002 in *Biological Psychology*, scientists compared three groups of meditators: those who had recently learned, those practicing for seven years, and those reporting consistent experiences of witnessing during waking and sleep. The witnessing group had been practicing Transcendental Meditation for 24 years, on average. The results of this study confirmed the previous findings. Higher frontal coherence, greater alpha power, and more general alertness were found in the subjects who had been meditating longer. The witnessing group in particular demonstrated a unique style of brain functioning in activity that was calmer and more efficient. [9]

These studies seem to indicate that the coherent brain functioning enlivened during meditation is progressively stabilized, resulting in expanded access to the brain's full potential during activity. Practically speaking, for the individual this means steadily increasing creativity, ability to fulfill desires, and increased efficiency.

The collective results of the research also indicate that for many of the subjects transcendental consciousness—the fourth state of consciousness—was becoming integrated with waking, dreaming, and sleeping states, providing objective and scientifically measurable evidence of the development of cosmic consciousness.[10]

The blossoming of cosmic consciousness in individuals practicing Transcendental Meditation is further indicated by: a more restful style of physiological functioning during activity (lower heart rate and breath rate); heightened wakefulness and alertness, as seen through increased coherence in brain functioning throughout the day; faster recovery from stress; and greater stability of the autonomic nervous system throughout the day.[11]

Another groundbreaking study, by Dr. Fred Travis and Dr. Harold Harung, was published in the journal *Management Decision* in 2009.[12] Drs. Travis and Harung studied Olympic and world champion athletes as well as top-level managers and world-class performers in many different fields—sports, government, business, art, and music. The research concluded that top-level athletes and managers could be distinguished from others by specific common features of how their brains and minds work.

Describing the research, Dr. Harung explains that in addition to having higher brain integration, these successful individuals also have a more mature psychology or higher moral development; higher morale; more frequent peak experiences in life; and more "luck" than the other group—people working at lower levels of performance or administration. Dr. Harung concluded that these differences are at the basis of the high performers' success. He added: "Both high-class businessmen and high-class athletes had greater ability to focus on what was important for the successful results of their action."[13]

Drs. Harung and Travis found that the greater levels of brain integration and psychological maturity these high performers display are also developed in people who have been practicing Transcendental Meditation for about seven years. It would be very interesting to see how much more brain integration could develop in these already world-champion athletes and top managers if they took up the practice of the Transcendental Meditation technique.

The studies I have briefly touched on in this chapter relate mainly to the growth of transcendental consciousness and cosmic consciousness. There are many more studies that show the benefits of Transcendental Meditation for all aspects of health. These have shown decreased stress, reduced incidence of disease, reduced hypertension, reduced cholesterol and lipid peroxides, reversal of atherosclerosis, reduced enlargement of the heart, reduced risk of diabetes, reversal of the aging process, etc., in those practicing TM.[14] All these studies further demonstrate the normalization of physiological functioning brought about by the deep rest gained during the transcending process.

Many people have been practicing Transcendental Meditation for many years now—30 to 40 years—and more research will be conducted that explores the continued growth in the direction of developing our total potential—unity consciousness. However, it is clear that the research completed to date shows a steady and highly significant development of brain potential through the regular practice of Transcendental Meditation.

Soon we will be able to have an entry/exit "Brain Integration" progress report[15] in every school, business, government office, and even prison, tracking the neurophysiology of enlightenment—how much each student, employee, staff member, or prisoner is developing their full potential. Governments spend almost as much money on maintaining a prisoner as it costs to send someone to Harvard, yet they put the prisoner back on the street even more stressed than he was before confinement. Prisoners could use their time behind bars to be effectively rehabilitated. They can focus on development of higher states of consciousness, not only for their own growth, but also for the improvement of society as a whole. Better yet, if we introduce Transcendental Meditation to students at a young age, I am sure we could dramatically reduce the number of people incarcerated in the first place.

This poem expresses an experience of how the body settles down during transcendence.

A Timeless Moment

My breath has become breathless
as I merge with the stillness of the gentle hour—
the holy time is hovering everywhere
my heart no longer beats yet has a power
of purest love flowing here and there.
I feel fully blossomed like a flower
dancing in the evening air.
The universe, my soul, my mind
are one harmonious song that shares
the sweetness—the rhythm beyond all time.

Experiences

I started Transcendental Meditation at age 10. I'm now in my late forties and have enjoyed many benefits of TM at every stage of my life. Almost constantly, my consciousness feels rich and full, illumined from within. I experience waves of bliss, as if the cells and tissues of my body are really pleased with life. Often when I'm just doing simple activities like driving or doing chores, I feel a sense of well-being that is not associated with anything in particular. It's an inner fullness of heart and peace of mind, but also a tangible, physical experience.

This experience has grown over the course of my life and continues to grow and become more permanent as time goes by. I know it's a result of my TM practice, because during meditation I feel that deep, nourishing quality in its most concentrated state, and then gradually it has become infused into my everyday awareness in activity. I feel deeply connected to nature—like a fish made of water, swimming in water. The world around me seems to be an extension of my own consciousness, and this is very fulfilling.

O.C.—North Carolina

At times during my practice of Yogic Flying golden liquid seems to flow through my body. It removes any stresses or strains from my physiology, allowing my joints and muscles to move almost without friction or resistance. Any ache or soreness that was there just a moment before is now gone. Only light and bliss remain.

S.D.—Canada

Recently during my practice of Transcendental Meditation I experienced transcending more deeply than I ever have before. The feeling of complete relaxation and contentment was so charming that I felt like there was nothing left to do. I could have stayed in that state forever. I felt softness expanding out from my head and it seemed like the structure of my body became lighter.

W.M.—England

11
BLISS

"Nothing from outside can stop a man from enjoying lasting peace and permanent joy in life, for it is the essential nature of his own soul."[1]

—Maharishi

My sister once asked me, "Why do you always use the word bliss?" It made me realize that most people have experiences of happiness, peace, and contentment, at least occasionally, yet many cannot relate to the word *bliss*.

Right from my first meditation, I experienced pleasantness, which in time has grown into something that I can only call bliss. There is really no other word to describe the experience of my consciousness becoming so melted and superfluid, so full, so vibrant, so peaceful. Often I am deep in meditation when suddenly I see thick waves of light start to flow within my awareness. Sometimes the flow is very gentle, and sometimes it is like a floodgate that opens up as thick waves of scintillating bliss flow through my awareness and body. There are even moments when I experience a state of pure ecstasy during meditation in which I just want to continue on and on. However, some responsibility or hunger will eventually bring me out!

There is a verse from the Vedic literature, in the Brahma Sutras (1.1.12), that says, *Anandamayo'bhyasat*—"bliss becomes blissful through practice." This is a common experience of those who have been practicing Transcendental Meditation regularly; the state of pleasantness and peace experienced when one first starts to meditate grows more rich and full with time.

My favorite Vedic verse is from the Taittiriya Upanishad (3.6.1):

Anandaddhyeva khalvimani bhutani jayante
anandena jatani jivanti
anandam prayantyabhisamvishanti

Out of bliss, all beings are born,
in bliss they are sustained,
and to bliss they go and merge again.

Maharishi has said that there is no reason why life should not be lived in perpetual waves of bliss, because bliss is the essential nature of our own Self, just as it is the essential nature of all life, as the ancient Upanishadic verse above simply states.

Maharishi describes transcendental consciousness as a concentrated state of absolute bliss consciousness. He has compared this state of bliss to the fullness of the ocean and our typical experience of happiness to the ocean's ever-changing small waves. "Outside is the joy of the drops of water; inside is the joy of the ocean of water."[2]

There is also a verse in Chandogya Upanishad (7.23): *Nalpe sukham asti bhumaiva sukham,* which translates as, "There is no joy in smallness. Joy is in the infinite, joy is in *Brahm.*" *Brahm* means wholeness of life, fully awake in one's unbounded transcendental awareness. The joy of transcendental consciousness is the only experience that can perpetually satisfy the quest in life to discover and dwell in the "big"—the totality of existence.

As explained in the previous chapters, we can experience this boundless sea of bliss during Transcendental Meditation, and we begin to move, or stir, our inner ocean of bliss through the Transcendental Meditation Sidhi Program. With regular practice, this concentrated state of dense bliss starts to become more and more fluid until it becomes as if completely liquid. Maharishi likened this experience to a potter working on a piece of clay. At first the clay is very thick and difficult to mold into a desired shape. As the potter kneads it steadily, the clay becomes more pliable, until eventually it becomes so soft that it will move in any way the potter wishes to shape it.

On occasion during Transcendental Meditation, I experience that my heart opens up and waves of thick bliss flow out of my heart. To me, this is the most pure, intense—yet tender—experience of bliss and love one can have in life.

Swetashwatara Upanishad (6.20) says: "It would be easier to roll up the entire sky into a small cloth than it would be to obtain true happiness without knowing the Self."[3]

The Taittiriya Upanishad (2.8.1–4) explains the extent of bliss that can be experienced by essentially saying: If you were a good, vital, intelligent, energetic person in the prime of life, surrounded by great wealth—all the wealth the earth had to offer—and if you consider that joy to be one unit of bliss, it would be only a minute fraction compared to the bliss of an enlightened person (up to 100 quintillion times more bliss, if calculated out!).

Having grown up in Palm Beach and the Hamptons, I found it interesting to meet many people who really have the best materially that life has to offer, yet so many of them are unhappy, have unhealthy addiction problems, and are spiritually unfulfilled.

On the other hand, in my travels around the world, I have met people who live simply with very little material possessions, yet are literally singing with happiness. Of course, I have also seen addiction problems in those countries and the struggles that go along with the woes of poverty. The point here is that true happiness is a state of being that anyone can have, no matter what his circumstances.

When Maharishi began teaching Transcendental Meditation around the world, his primary message was to refute the understanding that life is a struggle and suffering is normal. Rather, he proclaimed that the purpose of life is the expansion of happiness, and it is not necessary for anyone to suffer.

One can argue that bad things happen in the world and therefore suffering is a necessary part of life. Certainly, if you are not anchored to the silent, blissful depths of your own Self, you will be tossed about by the rough storms that sometimes appear in life. However, if you are established in the experience of bliss consciousness, you will not be blown over by any wind, however strong, that comes along. You may feel some momentary grief, sorrow, and the like, but the underlying presence of bliss naturally washes off these emotions and you are easily able to move forward in life.

In summary, Maharishi has said:

> The message of bliss has been the message of all the great Masters of all religions of all times. Christ said 'The Kingdom of Heaven is within you.' Buddha gave the message of *nirvana*. The Upanishads speak of the same *sat chit ananda,* eternal bliss consciousness, that is your own Self.[4]

All these great teachers speak of a higher state of human potential—enlightenment—and identify it as a state of pure bliss consciousness. This poem expresses my experience of bliss flowing inside.

Nectar of Consciousness

As I spiral in Self's inward turn
to point within the silent whole,
Thy nectar of bliss is smoothly churned—
holy waters rising from my soul.

As awareness awakens to Self-observation,
primal perception creating primal flow
stirs silence into gentle vibration,
frequencies, sound, form, in sparkling glow.

The infinite points warmed by Thy light
unfreeze Thy juice of bliss, oh endless Giver,
as waterfalls pour from mountain heights,
or snow melts into rushing rivers.

Drinking the sea of holy wine
dripping from each nectarine pulsation,
rivers of ambrosia of the Divine
rush in all directions, delighting in Self-oblation.

Sweetest nectar of consciousness
life-sustaining bounteous food,
ever-flowing within my fullness
fills me with silent beatitude.

Experiences

During my Yogic Flying practice I started to feel bliss on my skin, like some kind of very fine substance. As the practice continued this bliss started to permeate more into my muscles and lungs, so that every breath was experienced as bliss and every movement of my body felt like vibrations of bliss. My body felt lighter and less substantial; at times I wasn't really aware of my body at all unless there was some kind of movement in which case this movement was experienced as bliss.

W.G.—England

For the past couple of years, as a result of my practice of Transcendental Meditation, I have had an underlying quality of blissfulness, pretty much permanently. When I close my eyes during meditation I often see light that is brighter or darker depending on the intensity of blissfulness. The blissfulness is throughout my physiology and beyond, but particularly centered around the heart area. Last night this happened but there was a shower of light, like a fountain out the top of my head, which was very pleasurable. I then became aware that all the planets and universes were emerging from my head and spinning in ever widening circles. I felt I was the centre of all creation.

A.A.—England

Sometimes I am aware of a beam of light coming from my forehead between the eyes. What has pleased me most is that the subtle energy that was awakened at the base of my spine many years ago and is now mainly in my head has finally begun to enter my heart creating more waves of bliss.

S.C.—England

12
IN LOVE

"The strength of love makes one tender and firm, makes one weak in wrong and powerful in right, brings forgiveness in authority and grace in all fields of life… Fortunate are those whose hearts flow in love."[1]

—Maharishi

Have you ever noticed while listening to the radio that almost half the songs are about falling in love and being in love, while the other half are about breaking up or a broken heart? Love today, gone tomorrow! Poets, writers, singers, and scriptwriters depict the timeless, mysterious, yet universal topic of love in their respective fields of art. One of the all-time great songs made famous by Whitney Houston, called "The Greatest Love of All," talks about the supreme love that exists within everyone. Here is a verse from the song:

I found the greatest love of all/ Inside of me/
The greatest love of all/ Is easy to achieve

Everyone hopes to experience perfect love at some time in life—to be loved completely and to be able to love fully. The first experience of love is on the lap of mother. From that sweet seat of protection, nourishment, and affection, love spreads out in diverse ways. We love our different family members; we love our friends; we love our animals. We often feel adoration or love for the beauty of nature. We may love music, art, the written word. Religious people from all religions adore God as the purest and highest form of their love.

All these expressions of love are dependent on someone or something from the outside. Relying on a person or a situation on the outside for our love to flow towards is an unstable form of love, as the outer value of life is always changing.

In addition, due to stress and strain from overwork, tension, and fatigue, many people often feel restricted in their ability to love and are only able to love isolated objects or individuals. If you are no longer receiving joy from being with the person you love, then the current of love stops flowing.

There are so many situations in life that cause stress—pressures of work, financial hardships, lack of love and attention as a child, etc. In marriage, people tend to look to their spouse for fulfillment. If that fulfillment or support does not come—which it cannot if one is not full and content within—then tension and dissatisfaction develop in the marriage. When we are feeling stressed, we often take out those negative feelings on those closest to us, leading to arguments which can eventually destroy a relationship. Obviously, if one is more fulfilled inside, there is a much greater chance for a marriage, or any other relationship, to be sustained.

"Love thy neighbor as thy Self" (Leviticus 19:18) is a well-known expression from the Bible. My interpretation of this verse is that only if you love yourself and are completely fulfilled in your Self will you be able to love another completely. God is no exception here. Someone gave me a card once that included the following quote, which further develops this idea: "As the Self of all, the Lord is loved by all, with a love with which each person loves his own Self."

Love is an experience of the heart flowing. A child can melt the heart, music can melt the heart, and of course the experience of falling in love is a tender experience of the heart flowing. Wouldn't it be wonderful to wake up every day and just be "in love," not with anything or anyone in particular, but just as a daily experience of your own being?

The most profound experience of love is the experience of the transcendent. In his book *Love and God,* Maharishi says: "The hearts in whom universal consciousness has dawned are able to have the force of the unbounded ocean of love, even in the streams of personal love."[2]

Meditators commonly report that the heart as if physically opens and that they experience a gentle flow begin to pour throughout their body and out into the world. As a result of the deep rest you receive during the practice of Transcendental Meditation, deep stresses that have blocked the flow of the heart begin to dissolve. You then begin to enjoy the ocean of love in the depths of your inner silence, and in time that ocean of love begins to rise in waves of love within yourself. Then, like a cup overflowing, this love increasingly flows into the environment.

The flow of love is the flow of bliss consciousness and is actually what connects one with everyone and everything in the environment, since it is the essence of life and the most unifying force of life. In the state of enlightenment, unity consciousness, love for all creation is a natural and spontaneous daily reality, not an intellectual concept.

In this poem, I expressed my own feeling of pure love growing in my life:

Supreme Love

My love is touching all creation
with warmth of tenderest feelings,
returning to Self in Self-adoration,
lover and loved congealing
into oneness, then spreading apart
for love to always flow
as streams from a melted heart
where knower loves to know
Self as untainted love itself,
for Self is love divine.
Supreme love in silence dwells,
knower and known entwined.
Lover, loving, loved merged in lovingness
know deepest intimacy;
where one is the other in tender Beingness
ever united in ecstasy.
In unity, trinity sweetly conceives
love true and pure,
no need to give or to receive
in eternal love secured.
Then love loves for loving's sake
as a flower that blooms,
flowing endlessly as river to lake
for Self-love is never consumed.
To love my Self is to love everything,
all life sweetly embraced,
self-sufficient, unbounded, and free—
overflowing in God's grace.

Experiences

I experience that transcendental consciousness is like a substance; it has a texture; it is like being submerged in the depths of the ocean. It is indescribably soft and smooth. It is a field of pure love. Once during Yogic Flying a whirling pool of golden light opened in my heart. As the experience of silence deepens, and the enlivenment of the divine wholeness of life increases, I feel a melting of the small individual ego into the cosmic Self.

B.B.—England

One evening, after my meditation program, I had an exceptionally wonderful feeling; I was basking in love within and without. I felt love and sweet happiness all over; there was also excitement, just like the feeling of falling in love for the very first time. I slept like a baby that night, like a baby in mother's embrace, so secure and content.

W.W.P—Malaysia

During my meditation I often find my heart swelling in unconditional love. This is not love for someone or some object—it is pure, unbounded love itself. It is a knowing that, at the deepest level of consciousness, there is a field of pure love. When my eyes open after such an experience, it is as if everything is bathed in that love and I know that everything's essence is that love. At times my heart swells so much I find myself saying, "I love you." It is not that there is anyone there to whom I am saying this, just a universal sense of the loving nature of the universe itself.

L.G.—New York

At the end of my Transcendental Meditation practice my awareness felt as if it contained the whole cosmos, and this was followed by a sense of immense love and wonder. Then I began the Transcendental Meditation Sidhi Program, which nourished and brought light to many different dimensions of that inner being. My practice of Yogic Flying was lighter than before—more effortless, more blissful.

B.G.—England

13
THE WORLD IS AS YOU ARE

"If you are unified, your world is "uni." If you are diversified, your world is diverse. It is a viewpoint."[1]

—Maharishi

Recently someone sent me an email with the following parable:

TWO WOLVES
One evening an old Zarthosti told his grandson about a battle that goes on inside people. He said, "My son, the battle is between two wolves inside us all. One is Angre Mainyu. It is anger, envy, jealousy, sorrow, regret, greed, arrogance, self-pity, guilt, resentment, inferiority, lies, false pride, superiority, and ego. The other is Spenta Mainyu. It is joy, peace, love, hope, serenity, humility, kindness, benevolence, empathy, generosity, truth, compassion and faith."

The grandson thought about it for a minute and then asked his grandfather: "Which wolf wins?" The old Zarthosti replied, "The one you feed."

The Bhagavad-Gita brings out a similar point: "Let a man raise his self by his Self, let him not debase his Self; he alone, indeed, is his own friend, he alone his own enemy."[2]

My parents always told me you can either be sad that the glass is half empty or be happy that the glass is half full. I am sure everyone has heard this little piece of wisdom. What we put our attention on grows in our life, and if we put our attention on positive uplifting events, more positivity grows. However, if you are really upset about something, this can be difficult to do.

If you are feeling possessed by any of the qualities of the inner wolf "Angre Mainyu"—anger, envy, jealousy, sorrow, regret, greed, arrogance, self-pity, guilt, resentment, inferiority, lies, false pride, superiority, and ego—it is true that the outer world around you also reflects those qualities. However, if you *try* to have a positive attitude when you are actually feeling bad, this can cause strain and even more frustration. It also fosters a false sense of "mood making," which creates an uncomfortable feeling in the air among those around you.

All these negative qualities are due to stress in the mind and body. Stress weakens the entire system and can make one feel jealous, sad, insecure, etc. If we are feeling sad or angry, then the world around us also seems sad and angry. On the other hand, if we wake up feeling happy or had a good day at work or a great game of golf, then suddenly the world around us seems to be smiling. Outer life is a reflection of our inner feelings.

Joy, peace, love, serenity, humility, kindness, benevolence, empathy, generosity, truth, and compassion are all qualities of transcendental pure consciousness, because the transcendent is evolutionary, life-supporting, and all-nourishing. The more we experience pure consciousness through the practice of Transcendental Meditation and the Transcendental Meditation Sidhi Program, the more we infuse all these positive qualities of pure consciousness into our awareness.

Very naturally and spontaneously our nervous system is restructured to support the experience of pure consciousness more and more. The system actually becomes stronger. When we meditate and then plunge into activity, little by little we bring the qualities of joy, calm, compassion, etc. into our activity.

The important point is that there is no *trying* to change our thinking, no *trying* to feel happy, no *trying* to get rid of our ego, no straining to feel calm, no auto-suggestion. Naturally, the happier we feel and the calmer we are, the more life around us also reflects those qualities. We become stronger individuals and spontaneously begin to see the cup as full.

There is a self–referral loop that circles around us in our life. If we are negative and project that negativity out into the environment, then we are fed back negativity, which can make us feel even more negative. Likewise, if we are feeling happy and project that happiness out into the world around us, then that happiness reflects back and makes us feel happier. Dipping into pure consciousness is the best possible way to feed our self with happiness. It is like a well of joy we can drink and enjoy every day. Over time we really can become a cup overflowing with joy. It is no longer just seeing the cup half full—it is actually living life with the cup more and more full.

My father always told me, especially if I were complaining about a situation in school, "Life is what you make it to be." It is not the outer value that matters but what you make the outer value to be. Whatever we put into our life is exactly what we get back. The Bible (Galatians 6:7) says: "as you sow so shall you reap." In Eastern traditions this principle is called *karma*. In physics, Newton's Third Law of Motion similarly states that every action has an equal and opposite reaction. The outer just reflects back our own inner thoughts and actions. The more we experience the transcendent, the more our life will reflect its pure and divine qualities.

There is a quote in the Shwetashwatara Upanishad (2.14) that says: "Just as a mirror shines bright once it has been cleansed of dust, so those who have seen the Self shine in body and mind. They are always and forever filled with happiness." There is another Vedic quote that says: *Yatha drishtih tatha shrishtih*: "However [your] viewpoint, such is [your] creation."

I would like to end this chapter with a poem that reflects what this Upanishadic verse says. In the next chapter, "The Secret Beyond *The Secret*," I will go more deeply into this concept of "the world is as we are" and also explain how natural law functions to effortlessly fulfill our desires.

The World Is As We Are

Our mind is the creator of our world—
thus creator and creation are one.
The world is our own thoughts unfurled
creating rough waves or the calm ocean.

If we wear gray glasses we see gray—
the world is as we are.
Wear golden glasses and see a golden day—
the world shining as a brilliant star.

Our mind is like a window—dusty or clear.
Clear, it creates a world of gold.
Clear, it reflects Self's golden sphere—
a sparkling world for you to behold.

Clear the dusty window of your mind
by transcending to Self's transparent sea.
Then no dust can hide or bind
your Being shining its full glory.

Clearing our mind of confusions,
the Self sweetly reflects its purity,
dispelling mirage, dispelling illusion,
creating a world of God's divinity.

Experiences

Since the beginning, every time I meditate I find myself totally at home and secure. The deep peace and love that I receive from my own inner self is like a divine mother to whom I can surrender. Being enveloped by this loving softness, my heart expands and feels to embrace the whole world. Anxieties and doubts are dissolved and I know that I don't need anything from the outside to be full and happy. I experience myself as beautiful and divine, and the more I experience it inside, the more it radiates outside.

V.C.—Switzerland

Learning to meditate was one of the best decisions I made. I was real iffy before, but after going through the whole experience I'm really glad I chose to do it. It's given me so much patience. My body feels better, so rested, while meditating. It really takes a lot of stress away. It makes me more aware of what's around me, people-wise, and everything—I'm more conscious of what's going on. Certain situations that would have happened before I started meditating, and after, I would have reacted in two totally different ways. It really helps me to take time and realize what's important, to prioritize things in a way.

E.M.—New York

I experience happiness as a state of being rather than a feeling. My being is enjoying itself. It is churning, and churning, and churning, transforming my inner balance into overflowing happiness, love, and bliss. It is no longer a question of giving or taking. The kindness of nature embraces me.

P.P.—Denmark

14

THE SECRET BEYOND *THE SECRET*

"Progress and success is not achieved through hard work. Progress and success is achieved by training the mind to think from the deepest level, at the level of intelligence where thought sprouts—by training the mind to spontaneously think from that level where total Natural Law is lively."[1]

—Maharishi

My oldest brother is a very spiritual person and a deep thinker. Recently he said to my sister and me that it really bothers him when he hears people say, "God organized this. I was driving to the supermarket and there was a parking space, which God organized for me." He feels that no one from the outside organizes our destiny, but that we are responsible for what happens in our own life.

A few years ago a book and a movie called *The Secret* were released, which became very popular. The basic premise of *The Secret* is that our inner world creates our outer world—the situations in life in which we find ourselves are our own designs, created by the sum total of our thoughts, desires, expectations, and emotions. We project our own reality, and if we are not happy with what we have created so far, we can change it for the better. The secret of *The Secret* is that there is a law of attraction that is set in motion due to our thoughts; if we are happy and positive, we attract positivity and support from the environment. Similarly, if we are negative, we attract negativity and resistance from the environment. This premise relates back to the previous chapter, "The World Is as You Are."

The philosophy of *The Secret* adds another dimension to the reality of the outer reflecting the inner by also providing guidelines to achieve what you want. Again, the basic premise, or secret, is that we create our own successes or failures depending on the thoughts we have inside.

The philosophy of *The Secret* is in accord with my brother's basic belief that it is not something from the outside, not even God, that organizes our life; rather, our destiny is created by our own thoughts, feelings, desires, and actions.

Successful people spontaneously live the concept of *The Secret* and achieve what they want without even knowing the mechanics! The real achievers in life commonly display the same characteristic qualities. First of all, they clearly know what they want to achieve. They are also focused and persistent in achieving what they want and don't allow any obstacles that arise to deter them; and most importantly, they enjoy what they are doing. Thus, the laws of attraction that inspire success are set in motion, and they succeed in fulfilling their objectives.

Let's take the idea of *The Secret* to another level: "the secret beyond *The Secret*." The progress in quantum physics in recent years will help us understand this concept.

Scientists have been searching throughout time for the ultimate reality—a "theory of everything" that would unify all the diverse laws of nature. Einstein believed in and sought one single unified field of natural law—a set of unifying principles of nature's functioning.

In the twentieth century, classical physics systematically revealed deeper levels of order in nature, from the molecular and atomic to the subatomic levels. Probing even beyond the subatomic level of nature, quantum physics found that what appears to be solid matter is mostly space, eventually dissolving away into an abstract, unmanifest field. All activity in the universe can be reduced simply to interactions of four fundamental forces of nature—gravity, electromagnetism, the strong force, and the weak force.

In the last few decades, even these four fundamental forces have been proven to not be the ultimate reality. Through deeper understanding of the electroweak force and grand unification, scientists have discovered that the four forces are themselves composed of even more fundamental forces.

Recently, superstring theories have proposed that the four fundamental forces can be unified and are each simply excitations of one all-pervading field of unity—the superstring or unified field—from which all matter emerges. From the perspective of quantum physics, everything we see around us is composed of vibrations of an unseen, all-pervading field.

How does all this relate to "the secret beyond *The Secret?*"

In the early 1940s, physicists postulated that consciousness is somehow intimately connected with the universe. Max Planck, the first architect of quantum theory, declared: "I regard consciousness as fundamental. I regard matter as derivative from consciousness."[2]

In a similar vein, the English physicist Sir James Jeans wrote: "Mind no longer appears as an accidental intruder into the realm of matter; we are beginning to suspect that we ought rather to hail it as the creator and governor of the realm of matter."[3]

More recently, Eugene Wigner, a Nobel Laureate in physics, has said, "The next revolution in physics will occur when the properties of mind will be included in the equations of quantum physics."[4]

Right from the beginning days of his lectures on Transcendental Meditation, Maharishi often referred to the transcendent, or pure consciousness, as the home of all the laws of nature—the unified field of natural law. Maharishi delighted in conversing with leading physicists of the day, commenting on the latest theories in quantum physics. He would often point out the strengths of each theory and accurately predict the next layer of discovery. Maharishi would always correlate the most modern hypotheses of physics with the ancient Vedic science of consciousness. During the seventies, Maharishi expressed his satisfaction that physics had advanced to a level that revealed the unified field of all the laws of nature as a self-referral, self-interacting reality at the basis of creation:

> When the self-referral value of the unified field was discovered, we who had been practicing the Transcendental Meditation and the TM-Sidhi program immediately knew that the self-referral value of the unified field is Transcendental Consciousness. We experience that Transcendental Consciousness is the self-referral state of intelligence, the awareness which knows itself and nothing else. One's own Transcendental Consciousness, functioning within itself during the TM-Sidhi program, is the unified field functioning within itself. In the TM-Sidhi program, we practice that self-referral, self-interacting activity.[5]

The correlations that Maharishi made between quantum physics and Vedic science were remarkable; yet even more important is the practical significance of his Transcendental Meditation and Transcendental Meditation Sidhi Program techniques. When we align our awareness with the unified field of natural law during the practice of the Transcendental Meditation technique and then move and enliven that field through the Transcendental Meditation Sidhi Program, we are harnessing the support of all the evolutionary laws of nature that effortlessly conduct the whole universe.

This is reflected by a principle in physics known as the law of least action: any activity in nature always takes the path of least resistance.

In other words, the unified field conducts the whole orderly evolution of the universe effortlessly—most economically.

As Maharishi often put it: do less and accomplish more, do nothing and accomplish everything. Like an arrow on a bow, pull the mind back to the transcendent—the level of no action—and then you will have the full force of all the laws of nature lively in the transcendent to accomplish anything effortlessly. This is "the secret beyond *The Secret*."

A practical example, which I mentioned in an earlier chapter, explains how this works. I am sure you have sometimes had the experience of getting an exceptionally good night's sleep. You wake up feeling completely refreshed and happy. The whole day goes smoothly, and everyone seems to be smiling at you. This feeling of ease in activity is a growing daily reality for meditators, who not only experience effortlessness, but also the ability to fulfill the tasks of the day with focus and clarity, resulting in even greater success in activity.

This understanding of effortless action is the opposite of what many business leaders commonly expound. They say that, in order to succeed and move up in a business, you must work very hard—more than other people in the office: you must come in earlier in the morning, leave later in the evening, and even come in on weekends. Unfortunately, this strategy can lead to being totally stressed, anxious, and burned out, making you less effective at work.

If you are new to a job and want to prove your worth, there is certainly nothing wrong with going the extra mile. However, I would argue that someone who has a balanced routine, gets proper rest in the night, and takes time to meditate 20 minutes twice daily to rejuvenate and release the stresses of the day, will be able to accomplish far more in less time. He will be much more effective at his work and will also enjoy it more. To me, this is the ultimate win-win situation—the employer gets maximum creativity from his employee, and the employee gets improved health and greater happiness, as well as more satisfaction on the job. This also fulfills the popular dictum in the business world that says, "Work smarter, not harder."

This approach of maximizing the full creative potential of all the employees and avoiding burnout, both for oneself and one's employees, should be the new paradigm for success, not only in business, but also in education and all fields of life.

A growing number of top companies in many countries, including the U.S.A., Japan, and India, have introduced Transcendental Meditation for their employees as a corporate development program, with profoundly beneficial results. Extensive scientific research on the use of Transcendental Meditation in business demonstrates reduced anxiety, reduced worksite stress, decreased drug and alcohol use, lower blood pressure, and increased efficiency and productivity in employees, among other benefits.[6]

Also, many outstanding people have recently come forward to share the benefits of their practice of Transcendental Meditation, highlighting results such as increased creativity and improved well-being. They include Oprah Winfrey, Dr. Mehmet Oz, Paul McCartney, Jerry Seinfeld, David Lynch, Ellen DeGeneres, Clint Eastwood, Martin Scorsese, Donovan, Sheryl Crowe, Mike Love, Stephen Collins, Howard Stern, Russell Simmons, Laura Dern, and Russell Brand, to name a few.

As you regularly practice Transcendental Meditation, your awareness becomes more and more aligned with the home of all the laws of nature, transcendental consciousness. As time goes on, spontaneously you become more in harmony with all the laws of nature, and all actions automatically become more positive and evolutionary, not only for yourself but also for your surroundings. The key word here is *spontaneously*.

Fulfillment is based on action, action is based on thinking, and thinking is based on Being—pure consciousness. The guidelines of *The Secret* involve changing the thinking level—your attitudes and thoughts—by using techniques like positive thinking and vision boards. The approach of "the secret beyond *The Secret*" focuses on a deeper level. When you experience pure Being, your thoughts and actions naturally become more powerful. By transcending and accessing the home of all the laws of nature, Being, you *spontaneously* gain more and more support of nature to guide your success.

Maharishi often quoted from the Bhagavad-Gita: *Yogasthah kuru karmani*—"Established in Yoga [Being—the source of all the laws of nature], perform action."[7] The more your activity is infused with that silent level of Being—the home of all the laws of nature—the more smoothly and effortlessly every aspect of your life will flow in the evolutionary direction, leading to greater success and fulfillment.

I would like to give an example I am sure everyone has experienced. Have you ever noticed that when you are late and driving in a hurry to an appointment, you can easily start to become tense? It always seems that when you feel tense and in a rush, you hit every red light, you arrive at the bridge right as it is going up, or the train gate drops just in front of your car. You feel nothing is supporting you. Again, it is not that something outside is not supporting you, but rather that your awareness has lost its alignment with that quieter level of Being. If you are not in a hurry and feel relaxed, or even if you are late but maintain your equanimity, you seem to get all the green lights and everything goes more smoothly, so you end up arriving just at the right time.

Everyone has heard the expression "go with the flow." We can only "go with the flow" or be "in the zone" if we are in a relaxed and easy state, which grows naturally through the practice of Transcendental Meditation. To summarize, the "the secret beyond *The Secret*" is simple: transcend, and then spontaneously gain the favor of all the laws of nature to support your every intention for success in life.

How Nature Functions

How nature functions
one day all men must learn.
Nature's laws are for evolution.
For us, their wheels turn.
We may never know
all the various laws—
their source and how they flow—
yet into their home we can blissfully fall.
Then nature will gently carry us
on her effortless stream.
Life will be joyful, glorious
moving in evolution's scheme.
Then we will have truly mastered
the fine art of graceful living;
easily fulfilling what we are after
while growing in the ability of giving.

Experiences

Meditating is an overwhelming of joy for me. I used to be in a hurry to do everything, and get places and do this and do that and now after meditating I just kinda go, and it all seems to always get done anyway. I don't feel that rush, that pressure; I feel more calm. I can go with the flow and everything always seems to get done so I find myself just not being so stressed about things anymore. I'm there, and if they get done they get done and if they don't they don't, but they always do.

G.L.—New York

I feel very much connected to the world. A thought comes and shortly manifests ... a fulfillment of a desire expresses itself; someone calls or emails arrive; something I needed appears. I end each day with great gratitude for everything large or small that occurred.

K.S.—New Hampshire

Practicing Transcendental Meditation regularly has empowered me with the ability to fulfill my desires and goals without effort. All I do is have a desire or set a goal, be patient, and then just witness how everything gets organized towards the realization of that goal or desire.

R.M.—Puerto Rico

I notice more clarity of intellect. Decisions flow spontaneously in the best directions. Emphasis on "spontaneously"! It's as if my intellect is carrying out activity effortlessly and most efficiently. Years ago before I started Transcendental Meditation, in a perhaps lesser evolved state, I could never have organized anywhere near as beautifully as I am organizing now, simply because I am not so limited now, it's more that wholeness moving.

N.M.—California

After my TM-Sidhi course, I came back "floating" in the office. I felt very light and blissful when I was walking in the office carrying out my duties without any reasons to be happy, and I did not notice it myself until my boss's secretary commented a couple of days later. She told me that the boss commented to her that I am a totally changed person after my two weeks holidays. I suppose he must have noticed the glow on my face. They did not know that I had gone for my TM-Sidhi course.

T.C.M.—Singapore

15

THE MUSIC OF YOUR SOUL

"Music originates where unity starts to swing in the bliss of its own unbounded existence."[1]

—Maharishi

The power of music has always amazed me. Top singers and musicians attract thousands upon thousands to their concerts. I think it is fair to say that everybody loves music. It is a universal language that transcends race, culture, nationality, and religion. Every culture in the world enjoys its own unique style of music. I believe that music, more than any other art form, uplifts the spirit, makes one want to dance with joy, melts the heart, and touches the soul.

Why is music so powerful? As Beethoven put it, ". . . Music is a higher revelation than all wisdom and philosophy."[2] I decided to devote one chapter specifically to the topic of music and its relationship to the development of consciousness and enlightenment.

Have you ever wondered where music comes from? First, we need to ask, what is music? The dictionary defines music as "an artistic form of auditory communication incorporating instrumental or vocal tones in a structured and continuous manner.... It is sounds produced by singers or musical instruments."[3] The silence between each beat gives music its rhythm; the length of the silence along with the emphasis of certain beats form the different rhythmic patterns.

Of course, music is also found in nature—the sweet songs of the birds, the bubbling of a brook, the rushing of a stream, the whispering of the wind, the murmuring of the trees, the calming sound of the ocean, and the pitter-patter of the rain.

When considering the origin of music, the question arises, what is a sound? A sound is a vibration or frequency. The next logical question is, where do sounds come from? All sounds begin within silence and emerge from silence. It is a paradox to think that silence is actually composed of sounds—the primordial sounds of the universe—but it is true. In physics, superstring theory conceives of the elementary excitations of the unified field as strings or superstrings. Vibrating in different ways, they give rise to the fundamental forces of nature, including gravity.

The experience of transcendental consciousness is that of silence, but it is not a flat, empty silence. Your silence—your soul—is vibrant and humming. However, to hear these sounds you first must be able to hear the pure stillness of your own inner silence.

I'm sure you have had the following experience when taking a walk on a quiet summer evening. At first you do not notice any silence at all—you hear the sound of your footsteps, or you have many thoughts going around in your head. Then you come to a park bench and decide to sit down for a little while. After sitting for a minute, you become aware of the silence around you. Then after a few more minutes in that silence, you begin to hear crickets chirping in the distance, the leaves rustling in the wind, or the gentle rolling of the ocean.

This common experience is similar to the experience of transcendental consciousness. In the beginning, one may not notice the silence of the transcendent, but soon one begins to "hear" the stillness inside. After some time of practice, as perception becomes more refined, one begins to notice that the silence is alive—vibrant—with very subtle frequencies of sounds.

In the process of becoming aware of your own silence, there is a flow, a movement, a vibration. In the process of knowing yourself, there is a flow of awareness from you to the observed, which is still pure silence. This is the flow of silence within itself. Awareness opens to the eternal process of pure consciousness knowing itself—self-referral consciousness. In this perception of the Self becoming aware of itself, something very beautiful begins to happen—consciousness becomes lively and begins to vibrate or hum. All frequencies of sound are contained in the vibrations or humming of silence. This is where all sound begins; it is the music of silence, the music of creation, the song of eternity.

Maharishi says that: "Music is the flow of life, the flow of absolute Bliss Consciousness."[4] " ... every tone starts from silence, from the unmanifest field, and within each tone is the potential form for all possible subsequent tones."[5]

The great composer Johannes Brahms described his experience of silence beginning to vibrate as the first step in composing his music. Brahms not only experienced these primordial vibrations within silence; he experienced them as great joy:

I immediately feel vibrations that thrill my whole being ... and in this exalted state, I see clearly what is obscure in my ordinary moods.... Those vibrations assume the forms of distinct mental images, after I have formulated my desire and resolve in regard to what I want—namely, to be inspired so that I can compose something that will uplift and benefit humanity—something of permanent value.

Straight away the ideas flow in upon me, directly from God, and not only do I see distinct themes in my mind's eye, but they are clothed in the right forms, harmonies, and orchestrations. Measure by measure, the finished product is revealed to me when I am in those rare, inspired moods . . . . [6]

A branch of the Vedic literature called Gandharva Veda, which describes the ancient classical music of India, similarly explains how sound begins and emerges from the transcendental level of existence. Maharishi explains:

Gandharva music is the eternal melody of Nature, which is ever lively in Transcendental Consciousness. From there it reverberates and constructs different levels of creation.[7]

Every level of creation is a frequency. One frequency melts into the other, and this is how the process of evolution takes place. The night comes to an end and the dawn begins. At dawn, when the darkness and dullness of the night is over, some inspiring freshness comes, and there is a different frequency in the whole atmosphere. At midday, there is another big change in frequency; at evening, a different frequency; at midnight, a different frequency. This cycle of change is perpetual, and because everything is a frequency, there is sound at every stage... [8]

... there is a rhythm, there is a flow, there is an order in the rhythmic patterns of the evolutionary process in the universe.[9]

Explorer Richard Byrd, who lived alone for months in primitive conditions in subzero temperatures of the Arctic, experienced one evening not only unity with the universe, but also the fundamental rhythms and harmony that emerged from silence:

The day was dying, the night being born—but with great peace. Here were the imponderable processes and forces of the cosmos, harmonious and soundless. Harmony, that was it! That was what came out of the silence—a gentle rhythm, the strain of a perfect chord, the music of the spheres, perhaps.

It was enough to catch that rhythm, momentarily to be part of it. In that instant I could feel no doubt of man's oneness with the universe. The conviction came that that rhythm was too orderly, too harmonious, too perfect to be a product of blind chance—that, therefore, there must be purpose in the whole and not an accidental offshoot. It was a feeling that transcended reason; that went to the heart of man's despair and found it groundless. The universe was a cosmos, not a chaos; man was as rightfully a part of that cosmos as were the day and night.[10]

Aldous Huxley, the English writer, said, "After silence, that which comes nearest to expressing the inexpressible is music."[11]

The Sufi poet Hafiz obviously heard the music in nature as expressed in this poem:

I hear the voice
Of every creature and plant,
Every world and sun and galaxy—
Singing the Beloved's Name! [12]

William Wordsworth, my favorite poet, likewise perceived deeper levels of creation, in which a transcendent motion flows through all nature and even our mind:

And I have felt . . . a sense sublime
of something far more deeply interfused,
Whose dwelling is the light of setting suns,
And the round ocean and the living air,
And the blue sky, and in the mind of man;
A motion and a spirit, that impels
All thinking things, all objects of all thought,
And rolls through all things.[13]

In another poem, Hafiz said: "The voice of the river that has emptied into the Ocean now laughs and sings just like God."[14] My interpretation of this poem is that the "voice" is our own individuality, and the "Ocean" is the universal field of pure silence. When one transcends, one hears the music of silence, the music of God.

The Scottish writer Thomas Carlyle said, "See deep enough, and you see musically; the heart of Nature *being* everywhere music, if you can only reach it."[15] Fortunately, through the practice of Transcendental Meditation, we can reach the heart of nature, the tender delicate impulses of the music of nature, which is the lively silence of our soul, our own Being.

Maharishi says, "Since music is the flow of consciousness, the flow will be as delicate as the purity of the musician's consciousness."[16] Maharishi advises musicians that:

> The most important aspect of a musician's life is the delicacy of his own emotions. As stresses are dissolved and purity of consciousness grows through the practice of the Transcendental Meditation technique, the heart and emotions begin to flow in very delicate impulses, and that is the beginning of the melody of life...[17]

> The musician's awareness must be so delicate as to be one with the impulses that constitute Cosmic Life, and then the thrills of music will be the song of eternity.[18]

> When the musician's awareness pulsates in that most delicate value of life, he has a purifying influence on the whole society.[19]

Maharishi Gandharva Veda® music, emerging from the basis of all order and harmony in nature, has that most purifying, harmonizing, and integrating influence on the environment. However, all music has an influence, whether positive, negative, or mixed.

We know now that music is a sound vibration. How is it possible for sound vibrations to produce a tangible influence that can bring about change on the objective level of life?

From physics we know that sound is a wave propagating through space and time. For instance, if someone plucks a guitar string, it resonates, or vibrates, which produces waves of sound that travel through the air until they reach our ears. Our neighbor in the next house may not be able to hear the sounds, but that doesn't mean the waves stop at the wall of our home. It simply means our human ears have a limited range of hearing and can only pick up certain frequencies.

For example, the air is full of radio waves, but unless we turn on the radio, we can't hear them. Similarly, the atmosphere is full of radiation of every kind: microwaves, ultraviolet rays from the sun, radiation from TV and cell phone towers, etc. We may not see the waves, but that doesn't mean they are not there. In fact, science is now discovering that simply the presence of these waves has a great influence on our bodies. Everyone is aware of the harmful effects of X-rays on the human body. In addition, cell phone radiation has been shown to alter brain functioning in a negative way; UV rays from the sun, while invisible, can burn our skin and even cause skin cancer. Thus, it is clear that waves, or vibrations—including sound—have a concrete influence on physical objects and can be either constructive or destructive.

The power of sound to produce changes in the physical world is amply documented by science. One clear demonstration of the influence of sound came from experiments on plants. Research around the world has shown that plants respond differently to different kinds of music. When pleasant music such as Bach or Mozart is played for some time during the day, plants respond positively by growing faster, fuller, and becoming healthier in every way. When loud, jarring, dissonant, or continual music is played, the same plants start to wither and die.[20] Other research has shown the power of music to promote healing in patients who are ill.[21]

Maharishi has said that the purpose of music is to establish harmony and unity in the midst of all differences. Every musician has the gift to be able to uplift life, and the more a musician's awareness is attuned with his own silence, the more his music will have a positive influence in the environment.

Many musicians, composers, or singers say that their music or singing voice is a gift from God. For instance, the renowned composer Leonard Bernstein once said,

In the beginning was the Note, and the Note was with God; and whosoever can reach for that Note, reach high, and bring it back to us on earth, to our earthly ears—he is a *composer*, and to the extent of his reach, partakes of the divine.[22]

The note is our own silence, and it truly is a divine note. The more we experience that level of silence, the more we partake of the divine, and the more our soul begins to sing. I wrote this poem to give voice to my own inner experience with music:

Music

Music takes you to a place
    larger than you—
a vast, vibrant space—
    magical and true;
where tender emotions
    rise and swell
forming musical notions
    from the divine well.
The more delicate your heart,
    the purer the sound,
the more effective your art—
    deeper and more profound.
Music takes you to silence
    where God sings.
Floating in His alliance
    eternal music springs.

Experiences

During my practice of Transcendental Meditation I sometimes experience a whirling silence, which I feel is existence itself reverberating. I perceive a hum of creation welling up, like a thousand tiny bells reverberating with the light of a thousand stars.

S.K.—Pennsylvania

Often, at any time during the day, I am aware of how vibrant and lively my inner silence is.   My silence has its own lively song—beautiful high-pitched frequencies weaving in and out of each other, pulsating with energy and creativity. I am aware that this underlying dimension of consciousness is spontaneously giving rise to all my thoughts, emotions and ideas and that it sustains my work with vitality and success.

J.C.—North Carolina

I have the experience during Transcendental Meditation and in activity of all the sounds—birdsong, human, and machines—being perfectly part of a whole, like a picture, each part contributing to the whole, as a perfect piece. Also sights fit into the picture, and I'm part of it too—outside it and within it. Everything weaves together. It's incredibly beautiful and I love seeing and hearing it all, as it flows around and through me. The bliss has a quality of happiness with gratitude.

M.M.—England

I cherish every drop of silence that I enjoy during meditation. The silence is experienced as a continuum flowing through all aspects of my program, into all of life at all times, like the continuation of the hum of creation. The silence is integrated into my Being and I no longer feel any separation from this silence.

A.W.—North Carolina

16
RELIGION, ATHEISM, NEW AGE SPIRITUALITY

"The fulfillment of religion lies in gaining for man that for which the word religion itself stands. 'Religion' comes from the Latin root 'religare,' meaning 're,' back; 'ligare,' to bind: or, that which binds one back. The purpose of religion is to bind man back to his source, his origin."[1]

— Maharishi

Religion has been with us since the beginning of civilization. I find it fascinating how different religions have emerged over the centuries. Hinduism is recorded to have emerged between 3000 and 1500 B.C., Judaism around 2000 B.C., Buddhism around 480 B.C., Christianity at the beginning of the Common Era, and Islam about 570 A.D. In the Far East, Confucianism, Shinto, and Taoism existed for millennia before the introduction of Buddhism; the great civilizations of Mesopotamia and Egypt also revolved around their religions.

What about the religions of Central and South America, the tribal societies of Africa and all the indigenous cultures? Every major civilization and native culture has its own form of religion or belief in a higher power.

I have great respect for all the different religions and cultural traditions and enjoy learning about each of them. I am far from being a religious scholar, but it is very clear to me that each religion is open to interpretation. Various understandings are seen within all the major religious traditions.

In the Christian tradition alone, there are Catholics, Orthodox, Mormons, fundamentalists, dozens of Protestant denominations, etc., each with their own angle and interpretation of the Bible. There are liberal, conservative, and Orthodox Jews, each with their own vision of Judaism. Among Jewish mystics are those who follow the

Kaballah, and also Hasidic Jews. Within Islam there are two main branches, the Sunni and the Shi'ia. There is also Sufism, the mystical path of Islam.

According to Maharishi, there are so many different interpretations of religion because "knowledge is structured in consciousness" and "knowledge is different in different states of consciousness." He observed that the enlightened prophets of each religious tradition spoke from their fully awakened state of unity consciousness, but their followers listened from the ordinary waking state of consciousness. So over time, as the gap between teacher and disciples grew, the proper understanding of the religion was lost, and the essence of each religion—the experience of transcendence, the kingdom of heaven within, *samadhi*—was not experienced by the followers of each religion.[2]

I remember someone in my family once got upset with me because I did not go to church regularly. My response was, "Doesn't the Bible [1 Corinthians 6:19–20] say that the body is the temple of the Holy Spirit? I feel like I go to church twice a day when I meditate!"

I have been to many church services in my life. I find the teachings of the Bible meaningful, the music extremely uplifting, especially gospel music, and the sermons usually carry a positive message. However, I have never been to a church service where the congregation experienced transcendence. When I first learned to meditate, there was a Catholic Carmelite Father who came to the weekly advanced lectures given by the local Transcendental Meditation teachers in Oxford. He was a very kind, saintly person. He invited me to his Christian meditation class, and I went several times. He was very sweet and the class was uplifting, but the meditation was just a form of contemplation that kept the mind swimming on the surface level of meaning.

I have been to Buddhist and Hindu temples and listened to their chants, and I have also enjoyed listening to Christian Gregorian chants. Although I found the chants deeply settling and even experienced transcending during the chanting, in general the experience was not as profound as the pure experience of transcendence I enjoy daily during my practice of Transcendental Meditation.

Maharishi once addressed a major misunderstanding in the field of religion by saying that the *description* of the state of enlightenment brought to light in different religious scriptures is often mistaken for the *means* to gain enlightenment, or in other words, to reach God. In the preface to his commentary on the Bhagavad-Gita, Maharishi writes, "The state of Reality, as described by the enlightened, cannot become a path for the seeker, any more than the description of a destination can replace the road that leads to it."[3]

For example, in the Hindu and Buddhist traditions, an enlightened person is said to be unattached to the world and free from desires. As a result, many devout Hindus and Buddhists attempt to develop a detached attitude in whatever they do and also to suppress their desires. This is unnatural and only leads to strain.

In unity consciousness, our awareness is established in the non-changing state of pure bliss consciousness, and naturally we feel less dependent on the changing world around us. This does not mean that in order to reach unity consciousness you must try to become detached from everything. As Maharishi said in 1961:

We do not measure the growth of spirituality in terms of how much detachment has come to my mind, how much away from the practical life I have begun to be, how much less loving I have begun to be to my neighbors. No. The measure of the growth of spirituality is not an increase in the sense of detachment or renunciation, or less involvement in the world, or less interest in the world. The criterion of the growth of spirituality is how much I have grown in peace, in power, in wisdom, in creativity, in happiness.[4]

Maharishi said that trying to be unattached to everything you do in life only weakens the mind; it is unnatural and will not lead to a productive life. Desires are natural to life, and everyone should gain the ability to fulfill all their desires in a natural and spontaneous way. They are "stepping stones" of growth and progress, as the fulfillment of each successive desire leads to higher, more expanded desires. The more we unfold pure consciousness in our awareness, the more we gain the ability to fulfill desires, and the more evolutionary our desires become. In unity consciousness, we are completely fulfilled and are enjoying the goal of all desires.

According to Maharishi, the reason we see so much suffering and violence in the world today is because no religion makes available the effortless, blissful experience of transcendence. Maharishi upheld all religious traditions and always spoke very highly of Krishna, Buddha, Christ, Mohammed, and all the different saints and prophets. He encouraged people to go by their own religious and cultural traditions, pointing out that the knowledge of totality of life is present in each tradition. Every religious scripture mentions transcending.

Maharishi simply suggested adding Transcendental Meditation as a daily practice so that the essence of religion can naturally be experienced.

Some people believe that different religions are different paths to one ultimate God or truth. Other people believe their religion is the only way to God, and if you don't follow that particular way, you will not be saved by God or allowed beyond the pearly gates to Heaven. Other people believe that each religion is a different path with a different God or end result. Then there are atheists who don't believe in God at all and say there is no scientific proof that God exists. Some atheists believe that religion is a poison to life, citing as proof the Crusades, the endless wars of religion, the tragic recent events of 9/11, and other destructive events initiated in the name of religion.

On the surface level of life, the diverse opinions and debates among all these viewpoints can go on endlessly. However, there is one thing that is common to all humankind: whatever one's religion or lack of it, anyone who has the ability to think a thought can transcend. Everyone has the ability to experience transcendental bliss consciousness within.

Many ministers from all the different Christian denominations, Catholic priests and nuns, rabbis, Buddhist monks and nuns, and atheists have learned Transcendental Meditation. They find it does not conflict with, but rather enhances, their religious beliefs and practice.

Father Len Dubi, who has been meditating for 36 years, is a Roman Catholic priest from the Archdiocese of Chicago. Reverend Jonathan Chadwick, a Methodist minister also from Chicago, learned Transcendental Meditation in high school in 1975. Both men have spoken publicly in glowing terms about their own long-time TM practice, which they emphasized is not religious in nature, does not conflict with their religion, and only enriches their Christian faith. They said they meditate before their morning daily prayers and scriptural readings because it settles mind, body, and heart and makes their spiritual life more meaningful and fulfilling.[5,6]

Father Gabriel Mejia, a Catholic priest from Colombia and also a long time meditator, has introduced Transcendental Meditation into 47 shelters for homeless children. Many of these children come from a life of crime and have addiction problems. An extraordinary transformation takes place in the lives of these children after a short amount of time practicing the Transcendental Meditation technique. Their tormenting memories of living on the streets fall away, and they quickly recover from drug addictions. They begin to see the possibilities of a future for themselves, which gives them a newfound direction and purpose.[7]

Senior Rabbi Allan Green has publicly spoken about his experience of meditating.

> The first thing I want to say about my 37-year practice of the Transcendental Meditation program is that I never would have become a rabbi without it. Transcendental Meditation saved my Jewish life. How so? The short story is that in addition to its many other benefits, verified by over 300 scientific studies published in peer reviewed journals, the Transcendental Meditation (TM) technique gave me an experiential referent for the word, 'God.' Based on my own developing experiences with TM, I grew in love and appreciation for God, for His amazing universe, and for my own religious traditions. At the same time, I would emphasize that TM is truly universal, as anyone of any age, education, or background can practice it successfully, without any need for change in personal beliefs or lifestyle.[8]

Here is another personal perspective from a practicing Muslim from Egypt:

> I am a veiled Muslim who practices Transcendental Meditation (TM), and I cannot ever forget the first time I prayed after my first meditation. I learned the TM technique in December of 2006. I was speechless and cannot explain this state of complete serenity, contentment, and gratitude for God. TM increased my level of acceptance and appreciation for my faith and strengthened my beliefs.

> For example, reading from the Qur'an is becoming more enjoyable and comforting at the same time, as now I can better link its teachings with everything around me: my level of comprehension of its meanings is increasing on a daily basis. It is clear to me that the more I practice TM and the TM-Sidhi Program, the more deeply I realize different aspects of my religion and my mission in life.

> Finally, I would say that even though TM and the TM-Sidhi programs are not a religion and do not require any change in one's personal beliefs or cultural practices, they very well complement religion because they help to eliminate mental, emotional, and physical stresses and tensions. From my own experience I can say that the dissolving of stresses and tensions

purifies and strengthens the body, heart, and mind and results in a greater ability to live one's life in harmony with the highest goals of religious life.[9]

In Bangkok, Thailand, a Buddhist nun who is the principal of a girls' school has introduced Transcendental Meditation into her school. She was so enthusiastic about the results in her school that she attended a Transcendental Meditation teacher training course so she could personally oversee the daily meditation practice of her students and faculty. Many Buddhist monks have learned Transcendental Meditation in Thailand, and thousands of Buddhist monks in Japan and Sri Lanka are also enjoying the effortlessness of the practice.

What about all the New Age philosophies and techniques that are available on the market today?

First of all, I want to say that I have the deepest respect and appreciation for anyone on a spiritual path. I also believe everyone has to find a path that is most comfortable for them. However, it is important to ask the question, "Are all meditation techniques the same—do they use the same mental process, and do they produce the same results?" Science has shown that different meditation techniques produce different results. I would like to discuss some of the meditation techniques that are available today and how they relate to the experience of transcending.

Over the years, I have met many people who told me that they tried to meditate on their own and found it difficult; they couldn't settle down, they were restless, they were not able to empty their mind of thoughts, etc. This was so different from my experience of naturally settling down during TM that I realized that the word "meditation" is used to refer to many different techniques.

When most people think of meditation, they equate it with concentration. This common form of meditation involves focusing or concentrating the mind on a fixed object or thought. However, this type of concentration is unnatural to life and causes strain to the mind. As Maharishi explains:

It is wrong to believe that wandering is the nature of the mind. It is commonly held that the mind is like a monkey and to wander about is the nature of the mind, and because it is the nature of the mind it has to be controlled quite a lot through long practices in order to remain resolute. This is a wrong understanding...

Wandering is not the nature of the mind. The mind has been put in a position to keep on wandering, because there was nothing in its experience which could be so fascinating as to satisfy its thirst for happiness.... If there is any point of beauty, if there is any point of joy, it holds the mind. The greater the joy, the longer the stability of the mind on that.[10]

We all experience that if something is joyful, our mind naturally remains fixed on the object that gives us pleasure, without any effort to concentrate. So why is concentration thought to be an effective meditation technique? Sometimes it can happen, if one is concentrating on an object or a thought, that after some time of vigorously holding onto the object of concentration, the mind gets so tired that it lets go and opens to the transcendent, leading to a profound experience. For this reason, some people feel concentration is a means to transcend, but there is no way to repeat this experience regularly, so the aspirant often ends up worn out and dissatisfied. It is not concentration that allowed him to transcend, but rather the letting go. Why strain the mind if you can transcend in a natural effortless way?

Another common category of meditation involves contemplation (often called "insight meditation"), or meditating on a specific thought, idea, or theme. This process may collect the scattered mind, but it holds it on the surface level of meaning. Although this may have some settling and uplifting influence, in order to transcend one must experience progressively finer levels of thought until one reaches the finest level beyond thought itself—the source of thought, pure consciousness.

Prayer is also a form of contemplation, but usually we ask for something in a prayer or express a feeling of gratitude. Prayer can temporarily soothe or uplift our emotions. Maharishi once said that if you want your prayers to be more successful, first transcend to access the source of all prayer. Then, when you pray from that quiet, most powerful level of existence, there will be much greater ability for the prayer to be fulfilled.

One of the most popular meditation techniques today is mindfulness, known in the Buddhist tradition as *vipassana*, and often simply called "presence" or "being in the now." Some kinds of mindfulness meditations involve focusing on the breath; others involve being aware of sensations in the body; and many advocate simply being present to what is. In general, mindfulness brings the awareness inwards and has some quieting effect on the mind but does not allow the attention to effortlessly and systematically slip into the transcendent.

Perhaps the best-known practice today is yoga. There are many types of yoga available, and today it is considered mainstream. Even First Lady Michelle Obama presented yoga at the White House as one of the activities offered for children during the 2009 Easter Egg Hunt![11] Yoga postures have many health benefits and can both calm and energize the body and the mind, especially if they are practiced without strain. When most people today hear the word *yoga*, they only think of physical positions and stretches, but in fact, physical poses, called *asanas* in Sanskrit, are just one aspect of yoga.

The real meaning of *yoga* is "union"—union of mind, intellect, emotions, and body, and union of the individual with the universal. Transcendental Meditation singlehandedly takes care of integrating, or uniting, all these levels. When the awareness transcends and experiences the source of thought, it reaches the state of *yoga*—unity or *samadhi*—in which mind, intellect, emotions, and body are fully integrated.

The experience of transcendental consciousness or *samadhi*—"evenness of intellect" in Sanskrit—is the basis and ultimate goal of a truly blissful yoga practice. Many yoga asana practitioners who add Transcendental Meditation to their daily routine find it provides a deeply satisfying dimension of silence, awareness, and appreciation to their life as a whole; it also enriches their yoga practice.

Scientists are now studying different meditation practices and have identified three main types of meditation, distinguished by distinct brainwave patterns and mental functions. They have found that these different meditation techniques produce different results, as demonstrated in clinical trials.[12]

The three main categories of meditation identified by scientific research are "focused attention," "open monitoring," and "automatic self-transcending." Focused attention techniques include concentration and produce high frequency beta and gamma activity in the brain. This shows the brain is alert and highly focused, but not restful.

Open monitoring techniques include "mindfulness" meditation and produce theta activity, indicating more drowsiness in awareness. The practitioner may feel calm, but this quieter state of the mind is not clear and alert.

Finally, automatic self-transcending techniques, which include the Transcendental Meditation technique, are characterized by high degrees of alpha activity corresponding to relaxation and reduced mental activity (alertness without specific focus). As these studies clearly show, different meditation techniques have different effects on the brain.[13]

Dr. David Orme-Johnson, a prominent researcher in the field of meditation, states: "Over the 40 years that I've been interested in self-development, I've tried most of the meditation and relaxation techniques that are out there. In my experience, none of them do what Transcendental Meditation does."[14,15]

Other brainwave studies using EEG measurements have found that Transcendental Meditation helps the brain "reset" to a natural state of restful alertness—the "ground state" of mental functioning.[16] The practice of Transcendental Meditation also creates global EEG coherence, which means neurons in different parts of the brain are operating in synchrony, an indication that the total brain is functioning.[17] This integrated brain functioning has been correlated with peak performance in top athletes, managers, and government leaders.[18]

This scientific research by itself is a compelling reason to start Transcendental Meditation. I would also like to express several other reasons why I value and have continued with my practice of Transcendental Meditation and the Transcendental Meditation Sidhi Program over all these years.

First and foremost, my practice of Transcendental Meditation and the Transcendental Meditation Sidhi Program is an increasingly joyful experience. My inward experiences during meditation are becoming richer and more refined. Some days I become so absorbed in my meditations that time does not exist. The bliss has become a thick, dense, superfluid substance that I bathe in daily and which completely rejuvenates my body. My heart has become full to overflowing, and I feel happy all the time. I am continually experiencing positive changes in the outer values of life such as fulfillment of even the slightest desire. Life has become a magical, exciting play.

I feel confident knowing that Transcendental Meditation has been passed down in its purity through the Vedic Tradition of Masters from time immemorial and has thus withstood the test of time. It is not a technique that has recently been invented by any individual, as many of the other techniques available today have been. The extensive scientific research mentioned above further confirms and supports my experience, as it verifies the benefits I feel on all levels of my life: physiological, psychological, emotional, and in the field of social relationships. Research has also documented the broader influence of Transcendental Meditation for society and even the entire world. My experience is far from an isolated case: over five million people around the world have learned Transcendental Meditation and have experienced wonderful results from their practice.

Until Maharishi began teaching the Transcendental Meditation technique around the world, a clear understanding of the natural growth of consciousness was unavailable. Maharishi has provided the world with systematic knowledge of the seven states of consciousness that naturally unfold on the path of enlightenment. This knowledge has been so precious for me in understanding and appreciating the development of my inner experiences.

Transcendental consciousness, or pure consciousness, is the quietest level of everyone's awareness; as such, it is ever present as the basis of individual existence. Therefore, it is possible that anyone at any time can have an experience of transcendence through any type of meditation, or even by reading a book, listening to music, participating in sports, sailing on the sea, walking on the beach, or simply by doing nothing. Similarly, anyone can have spontaneous experiences of higher states of consciousness such as cosmic consciousness, God consciousness, and unity consciousness.

The point to note, however, is that although many people have spontaneous, fleeting experiences of transcendence and higher states of consciousness, the permanent state of enlightenment can only be developed in a natural and systematic way. Maharishi's contribution to the world, through his Transcendental Meditation technique, is that now anyone of any background can grow in enlightenment. Transcendence is often experienced even in the first meditation, and through regular practice and experience of transcendental consciousness, higher states of consciousness automatically develop.

As I mentioned previously, Maharishi has provided a comprehensive understanding of each step of the growth of higher consciousness. He always emphasized the importance of both knowledge and experience. You can own a diamond, but if you do not know its value you may discard it as a useless stone. You may be told throughout your life about the delicious taste of a mango—you learn all about it: its origin, nutritional value etc.—but until you actually taste a mango, you will not really know what it is.

We have all met people in our lives who we feel are very highly evolved souls. They may have an incredibly calm quality about them, or an extremely open and loving heart; they may be extremely wise, have an infectiously joyful personality, or all of the above. Someone once observed that one of my nieces was *born* happy, and we have all met people like that.

Whatever we do in our lives, we are always learning and growing; in other words, evolving. In terms of reaching the goal of life—to live the full value of our own consciousness—we can either move slowly or quickly along the path. To get somewhere quickly, we can choose to take a car, a boat, or a jet plane. Transcending regularly and effortlessly every day is like the jet plane of evolution. The sooner we experience the transcendent and stabilize that experience in our life, the sooner we will enjoy bliss consciousness—heaven within. Maharishi has always advised students to seek the highest first. The Bible (Matthew 6.33) says, "Seek ye first the Kingdom of Heaven ... and all these things shall be added unto you." If we are happy inside, then everything else in life is a beautiful, uplifting wave upon the flowing yet silent ocean of our inner bliss.

Self, the Temple

The Sabbath has come.
The bells are chiming.
Are not all days holy?
Is not Self the temple—
Heaven of the midday sun?

It is time for scripture,
To offer prayer.
Is not silence the sermon?
Is not bliss the Lord,
In one's Self ever secured?

The choir is singing,
The organ-master playing.
Are not the birds as joyful,
The wind as melodious?
Is not God everywhere ringing?

All are coming to hear,
To be redeemed.
Is not silence the soft sound
Where one is reborn in eternity
Attaining oneness intimately dear?

God speaks in silence—
Altar of the heart.
Is not one's Being divine—
The shrine of pure love—
Surrendering to which one gains alliance?

Experiences

During the Transcendental Meditation Sidhi Program, bliss bubbled up from within me. Deep inside my core was an unbounded ocean of bliss. Every in-breath was pushing it throughout my Being, throughout my physiology. My body became a vessel filled with celestial bliss. Thick golden light emerged from the underlying wholeness: fullness coming out of fullness, leaving unity. There was so much bliss, dignity and reverence, my heart opened to discover the divine. Surrendering into this peace and supreme bliss, a mantle of divine grace enfolded me, overtaking my entire Being, then radiating back out to the universe. This was the reality of who I am. I knew that this fullness of bliss is love, is the divine, the grace of God. I felt totally invincible with this overflowing heart.

T.G.—Canada

When I close my eyes during Transcendental Meditation the material world dissolves as the concepts of the mind dissolve, and I become what I am—the unbounded, eternal light of life. In that awareness, fully awake, I feel I am the essence of everything, the breath of life without movement, the light of God, full of light, without the sense of sight (functioning). The pure silence is yet full of the potential dynamism of life. I am ageless and eternal—the source of life itself. And when I open my eyes nothing changes, I remain that essence.

K.D.—Vermont

There have been times both in and out of Transcendental Meditation when my physiology was completely at one with the Universe. I experienced more and more light in my meditation, sometimes witnessing it but mostly it becoming a part of me.
Three days ago, when I was very deep in the transcendent, I saw brilliant white light. I had a deep feeling of peace and realization that God was present in me. Now in meditation and in activity I feel His presence.

A.A.—England

17

SELF-EMPOWERMENT AND WOMEN'S LIBERATION

"When the mind, through meditation, has become contented in the bliss of the Self, there is no possibility of discontent. Then there is evenness of mind in both pleasure and pain. Such is the state of a liberated man."[1]

—Maharishi

My grandmothers, my mother, and all my aunts fulfilled the traditional role of a wife and mother at home while their husbands worked. Growing up, I assumed my life would take this same traditional path. When I was around 16 years old I started to rebel, not so much about the role of women, but about certain superficialities of my upbringing. Going down to our summer club, I often felt like I was playing a particular part with the right preppy wardrobe to accompany my role— Jack Rogers sandals, Lily Pulitzer dresses, and bright cable-knit sweaters. I sometimes sensed I was being judged not by who I was as a person but more by whether or not I was properly fulfilling the role that was expected of me. I felt trapped by this and started to break away from this external pressure.

I also felt the conversations at our summer club rarely went beyond, "Hello, how are you, so nice to see you, what prep school are you going to?" I started to feel like a parrot always giving the same answer. When my parents had cocktail parties I had much more fun in the kitchen making the hors d'oeuvres and talking with those helping than being with the other guests. I noticed that the help never asked me any of the above questions and that they just were enjoying being with me, not trying to categorize me. They seemed to just be enjoying the moment. This made a deep impression on me. Much to my parents' chagrin, I refused to have a debutante party and opted to wear blue jeans all the time. However, this was just going from one image as a preppy to a different image. I was definitely struggling inside trying to find my identity.

When I began meditating I noticed that I started to feel more comfortable within myself. During moments of pure transcending, I experienced a very powerful state of being—my unconditional being—beyond any social expectation. This was a huge sense of freedom and relief. I started to feel stronger as a person and started to appreciate my own individuality. I no longer felt bound to follow a specific path, such as the one I had assumed I would take—the traditional and expected path of being a housewife and mother. Life became a field of all possibilities and I knew I could do whatever I wanted. It was a real experience of Self-empowerment and internal liberation.

Fortunately, women today have many more options available to them than ever before. In the past half century, a major societal development has been the increasing equality for women. Although there is still a ways to go, there has been tremendous progress in areas such as equal rights and equal pay, and in other inequalities women from almost every culture have endured and often continue to face.

There are many women's organizations, especially in developing countries, working to help young women and girls gain self-respect and become self-empowered, mainly through education. The present generation of women is extremely career-oriented. In fact, according to the National Center for Education Statistics, in 2010 more women than men graduated from college.[2] Today, women also play an increasingly significant role in the fields of business, government, and healthcare, using their expertise to help solve community and global problems.

Even though many women have been "liberated" from the home and are enjoying their careers, some women are confused about their roles or are trying to fulfill many roles at once. They want to have a career, be a supportive wife, be a mother at home, and take on community responsibilities as well. Unfortunately, for many women role-juggling like this often creates great stress, as indicated by the increase of heart attacks, divorce, dysfunctional family life, and so on.

A recent study found that middle-aged women are increasingly at risk for heart disease. Researchers looked at data on more than 4,000 middle-aged men and women from surveys conducted between 1988 and 1994 and then again between 1999 and 2004. Women's risk of heart attack rose from 0.7 percent between 1988 and 1994 to 1 percent in the recent period, while men's risk of heart attack decreased (from 2.5 percent to 2.2 percent).[3]

Having a job or career can be very tiring and stressful. Climbing the corporate ladder, building your own business, teaching, nursing, or engaging in any other profession requires stability, adaptability, mental clarity, and physical and emotional stamina.

Whatever lifestyle she chooses—a career, marriage, motherhood, or trying to do it all—the important point is that every woman should learn how to nourish herself from within, empower herself from within, and feel liberated from within. Liberation means, at the very least, being free from fatigue and stress, which can imprison you, weigh you down, and lead to poor health and unhappiness. Even in the common sense of the word, liberation implies that a woman must at least enjoy what she is doing. She must be in a situation that feels natural to her.

Unfortunately many wives today feel the opposite of liberation—trapped in an unhappy marriage. About 50 percent of all marriages today end up in divorce. That is quite a depressing statistic. I can't help wondering, how happy are the couples that are still married and trying to keep it together? Certainly there are some happy, harmonious marriages, but they seem to belong to rare, lucky couples.

One reason many marriages don't succeed is because each spouse is looking to the other for fulfillment. If that fulfillment does not come—as it cannot endlessly—then unhappiness and tension creep into the marriage until, before you know it, too many bridges have been burned and the marriage winds up in divorce. Obviously, if we are more fulfilled from within, more self-sufficient in our own happiness, then there is a greater chance for marriage to succeed.

If you take the time to meditate, you will find that stress dissolves and everything in your life runs more smoothly. Like many women, you may wonder, "How in the world can I possibly fit twenty minutes twice a day into my already incredibly hectic schedule?" There are many ways to fit Transcendental Meditation into your routine, such as when you take a bus or train to work, or during work breaks at the office.

Your children will be the first beneficiaries of your growing calm and patience. I have heard many stories of children noticing when their mother has missed her meditation and then reminding her to meditate so she would be nicer to them. You will also have extra energy to be more present and attentive to your spouse. In addition, people find that when they meditate, they are more efficient at work and can accomplish more in less time. Therefore, you will also be able to contribute more to your work environment.

The role of a mother at home is the most important role on earth for the betterment of humankind and for peace in the world.

Mother is the first teacher of the child, she is the rock of the family, and she is the main source of nourishment for the family. She has to balance all the diverse tendencies of each family member. By nature, a mother ceaselessly gives, often without taking adequate care of her own self. It is so important for every mother to take the time to meditate twenty minutes twice a day. If the mother doesn't feel peaceful and happy, how can she give those qualities to her family?

Peace begins in the individual, grows in the home, spreads to the community, then to the nation and the world. Every mother has to take the time to nourish herself from within, and then she will be able to create a peaceful environment in the home and nourish her family without draining herself.

To cope with the onslaught of daily stresses, women all too often turn to insomnia medication, caffeine, unhealthy diets, alcohol, and cosmetic surgery. These choices take a toll on the mind and body, accelerating the aging process. On the other hand, published research shows that just one year of regular practice of the TM technique can be a healthy antidote to stress and its detrimental effects. Even short-term practitioners of this meditation have, on average, a biological age five years younger than their chronological age. Five years of regular practice of Transcendental Meditation results in a biological age 12.5 years younger than the practitioner's chronological age.[4] Rather than having to do something as drastic as going under the knife or using Botox, which has undesirable side-effects, in an attempt to look younger, isn't it better to reduce stress, one of the major causes of premature aging?

Whether you are a mother or a career woman, to be fully liberated you must liberate the bliss lying dormant within you. Every person on earth has an ocean of bliss within, waiting to be tapped, waiting to be stirred, so it can flow like a river. Bliss flowing within and from our hearts to the environment is the greatest nourishing power that exists on earth. This is the cosmic role of every woman on the planet: simply to nourish and uplift the whole environment. The wonderful news is that assuming this cosmic role is the spontaneous byproduct of our own liberation.

A happy, fulfilled woman who knows herself and is comfortable with who she is has a great power to move mountains and help uplift her family and society. Our troubled world deeply needs the nourishing inner quality of every woman to soften the hardness that is prevalent everywhere today. Mothers, more than anyone else, have the ultimate motivation to create peace, as no mother would ever want to see her child go to war.

Every fulfilled woman will spontaneously assume the role of

peacemaker and embrace the whole world as her family. She will create peace from the level of peace itself, as another byproduct of the growing value of self-empowerment, liberation, and enlightenment. Peace from the level of silence, peace from the level of bliss, is the most practical way to create true and lasting world peace.

This poem expresses the experience of inner freedom, or pure liberation.

Caught

Becoming unbound
Cutting asunder the knots of matter
Escaping boundaries
Emancipated from relative fetters.

Finally free
From all binding connections
Moving unhindered
In prisms of omni-direction.

No longer immured
All restrictions joyously released
Only to be captured
In the bliss of Thy heavenly peace.

Experiences

Though I never had children of my own, I feel my motherly instinct has grown stronger with my practice of the TM technique. Often I am aware of the feelings of my friends, family, and students, and I intuit when they need support and encouragement, without them asking for it. I feel my consciousness radiating from my heart and mind like a tender net of love that powerfully envelops and nourishes whatever I put my attention on. I find that with the growth of inner fullness, vibrancy, and happiness, I am better able to offer help or companionship without needing anything in return.

J.C.—North Carolina

Within the first one or two minutes of my TM practice, I effortlessly sink into deep silence. I return to my own true Self, which is the source of creation. After my practice of TM, I am refreshed and renewed, which helps me to maintain balance and properly nourish my children and husband. Experiencing daily the silent, unchanging reality of the transcendent helps support the ever-changing and sometimes challenging circumstances of family life.

J.H.—Canada

When I meditate, thoughts and ideas in my head become clearer. Afterwards, I feel a sense of peace, and I find myself more open and accepting. It's easier to laugh, smile, and just enjoy.

C.P.—California

A few weeks after my instruction in the Transcendental Meditation program I had a clear and powerful experience of transcending. I closed my eyes to meditate and went to a very deep place within. It was like gently being dropped into a pool of unbounded and infinite SILENCE and BLISS. It was the most delicate and subtle and quiet place that I had ever experienced. There were no thoughts, but the feeling was like I had finally come home and experienced who I was at my most fundamental core, my true SELF. I have had many glimpses of this place of silence, peace and unbounded freedom over the years and have even had moments of the same while in activity.

J.B.—Iowa

18
MOTHER DIVINE – THE DIVINE FEMININE

"The word 'Divine' is associated with unboundedness. Liberation – eternal liberation ... When we say Mother Divine, we mean Mother of mothers. Mother of all that there is. All creation springs from that which is Mother Divine – Divine Intelligence. Creative. Protective. This is just Creative Intelligence."[1]

—Maharishi

A favorite experience of mine that has been growing since I learned Transcendental Meditation is of a soft, flowing feeling in my heart. Some days my heart feels wide open and I feel the many barriers and defenses that I had built up before have simply melted away. I can let go and be myself in simplicity and tenderness. On one level I feel more vulnerable, more sensitive, but I also experience this openness as a strength. I no longer need to put up an inner wall to shield me from getting hurt.

In these moments of complete openness, I notice I am more in tune with my real feelings. It is an experience that is incredibly satisfying, even *divine,* because it is simultaneously self-nourishing and outwardly nourishing. I equate these feelings with the most natural qualities of universal mother—a divine mother—the divine feminine.

You may have heard the expression "divine feminine" or "sacred feminine". The divine feminine is the goddess value that exists in all traditions. This value also reflects Mother Earth—symbolizing balance and healing, renewal and restoration. Divine feminine qualities include nurturing, loving, understanding, compassion, insightful, intuitive, creative, forgiving, healing, steady, patient, and wise.

The Vedic tradition of India uses another expression: "Mother Divine". Like the divine feminine, the term "Mother Divine" refers to universal, all-nourishing qualities of nature—bliss, intelligence, creativity, harmony—that exist within everyone and always promote life in the direction of peace and progress. Uncovering these inner qualities cultures the state of enlightenment. All we need to do is remove the stress and strain that covers our essential nature.

When we fathom the inner depths of life, we connect with our deepest self and simultaneously nourish the world around us. Nourishing the world means that you are able to soothe and uplift your environment without diminishing your own well-being.

As we grow in the awareness of the divine feminine within, we naturally appreciate the positive values in any situation and easily bring out the good and beauty in others. This is not contrived—you don't have to make positive affirmations or tell yourself "I'll be nice today" or "I am not going to let that person at the office get to me today". Spontaneously you grow in the ability to take recourse to your own inner strength, calm, and happiness; after all, that is who you essentially are beneath the layers of stress, hurt, and defenses you may have built up in life.

Being nourishing does not mean that you lose your ability to discern negative influences in the environment. In fact, you will become more sensitive to the rights and wrongs around you, and will be stronger and more able to favor the right and avoid the wrong.

Maharishi has explained that the tender feeling level is deeper than the intellect. It is the level closest to the transcendent. Transcendental consciousness is the home of the evolutionary power of natural law. When we access and stabilize the transcendent through Transcendental Meditation, our thoughts and actions naturally become aligned with this totally life-supporting power of nature and our intuition becomes more powerful.

Being in tune with this feeling level allows us to spontaneously act in harmony with the world around us. I am sure you have sometime had the thought, "if only I had gone by my own feeling". Those who learn to listen to those quiet internal whispers of the feeling level notice that their inner voice can powerfully guide them in the right direction.

When Oprah Winfrey interviewed Bishop T.D. Jakes, author of *Instinct: The Power to Unleash Your Inborn Drive* she mentioned that all her major decisions were guided by instinct. Oprah asked him, "how do we allow ourselves to be in touch with that which is instinctively there to help us to unleash the inborn drive?"

Bishop Jakes answered that all the noise coming from outside drowns out our inner voice: "We live in so much noise that we don't have time to hear what's coming out of inside …"

When we transcend and experience inner silence, all the noise we are daily bombarded with from the Internet, Facebook, Twitter, Instagram, television, etc fades away. Our awareness can reach the level where instinct, intuition, finest feelings, and even creativity emerge and our mind can perceive all these subtle values more clearly. Through regular transcending, this experience also grows in activity.

Every woman is born with these precious instincts and nourishing power as a natural part of her capacity to carry, give birth to, and sustain new life. If not protected, these tender instincts can be covered up or even vanish, especially when women are exposed to excessive fatigue and stress. Women who lose access to their essential inner nature struggle through many situations in life, and can become full of fear, distrust, and anger.

To enhance women's ability to be in touch with their inner strength and intuition and to enliven their innate nourishing power, a new wing of the Transcendental Meditation organization was established in 2007—the Global Mother Divine Organization (GMDO)—also known as the Global Women's Organization in some countries. An organization for women by women, GMDO aims to raise the quality of life of all women by developing their consciousness, their inherent "Mother Divine" spiritual reality, as well as by providing practical programs in the areas of women's health, education, culture, and music.

Enlightening women is a profound and fundamental means to bring effective change in society. Giving girls the experience and understanding of their own Self from a young age empowers them to easily nourish their family, friends, and the whole society. Girls who learn to meditate and have a tool to reduce stress grow up with great inner strength and brilliance without losing their refined, divine feminine nourishing qualities.

In 1981, 27 years before the Global Mother Divine Organization was established, Maharishi inaugurated the Mother Divine Program[SM]—an advanced program for single ladies—and a similar program for single men, the Maharishi Purusha Program[SM]. These programs are similar to an extended spiritual retreat and give women and men the opportunity to focus on developing higher states of consciousness through extended practice of the Transcendental Meditation and Transcendental Meditation Sidhi programs and a healthy balanced daily routine. Those participating in the programs accelerate their development of enlightenment—inner fulfillment, self-sufficiency, and 24 hours of bliss.[2]

I was very lucky to have joined the Mother Divine Program when it first began. I remember my first impression of being in a situation where there were only ladies—I could really relax and be fully myself. The incredibly soft, refined atmosphere of this group of ladies effortlessly dissolved the hardness of the outside world. It was a mutually beneficial experience. As we settled into the routine of enjoying longer and deeper meditations, the deep softness created by the group nourished all of us.

To date over 1,000 women have participated in the Mother Divine Program for some time. The minimum time requirement to join this program is six months. Many find that during the first four to eight weeks they eliminate a great deal of accumulated tiredness that had built up in the physiology over many years. Once that surface fatigue is gone, then the deeper, more fulfilling levels of bliss begin to open up. The remaining months bring clearer experiences of pure bliss consciousness, allowing one to stir and stabilize the ocean of bliss within.

Many women continue on the Mother Divine Program year after year, because the experience of bliss and peace is so full and charming. I remember one person who decided to join the course for the minimum time of six months. She mentioned that before she began the program, she had prepared herself to renounce her freedom for that half year. Instead, she experienced quite the opposite: she gained the true sense of freedom she had always desired.

After enjoying the Mother Divine Program for some time, many women leave to marry and or embark on a career. Everyone, without exception, deeply values their time spent on the Mother Divine Program, for they depart stronger, happier, more creative and fulfilled, with a solid inner foundation for whatever they want to do in the rest of their lives.

Every girl upon graduation from high school or college should spend at least six months on this program, especially before making important life choices. Her decisions will be wiser, her joy deeper, and she will have a much greater chance of success and fulfillment in whatever future direction her life takes. There are also options to earn a university degree while participating in the Mother Divine Program.

Shorter courses are offered on or near Mother Divine Program campuses for all women, including mothers, students, and professionals. The women who attend find the courses extremely enriching and rejuvenating—an ideal environment in which to sink deeply into the luxury of their own silence. I say luxury, as silence is a luxury in this fast-paced day and age. One mother who frequently comes to these courses said, "Attending courses in this refined atmosphere of all ladies is the best kept secret in all America."

After returning home from these courses, women report that they are able to give so much more to their children, husband, and coworkers, on the basis of the deep inner rest and fulfillment they have gained.

Soon, attending the Mother Divine Program for some time will be as mainstream as yoga and meditation, because bliss is so essential, fulfilling, and impossible to resist. Women everywhere are searching for more balance and meaning in their lives. They need only look within and experience their essential "Divine Feminine—Mother Divine" nature.

Divine Mother

Is She an illusion or is She real
So sublimely ethereal —
Appearing solid yet surreal?

Is She pure silence or is She motion
Or just a faint and joyous notion?
Is She Heaven or is She earth
Embracing the entire universe?

Is She star-laced nights
Or the moon's glowing light—
Our vision's sweetest delight?

Is She tenderness or is She powerful,
She who is invincible in gentleness—
Is She laughter or bubbling bliss
Enveloping all in wholeness?

Is She creation's diversity
Or is She life's unity—
Binding all differences in harmony?

She is all this, and even more—
She is the essence of what we live for.
She is in you, She is in me,
Shining forever divinely.

Experiences

I love coming to these courses at Mother Divine. Deep rest, deep experiences of a level I don't experience anywhere else. The silence is profound.

A.D.—Iowa

TM has been an extraordinary gift in my life. When I begin a session I have a beautiful sense of rising above the constraints of my mind and a feeling of release and freedom. In this place everything feels possible and warm and loving; I feel the struggles of the day melt away. TM has helped me grow into my true self. I feel more comfortable and fluid with my creativity and my vision. I am calmer and more focused in my daily life and have much more energy. The practice has also strengthened my commitment to doing what I can to make a difference in the world.

A.H.—Florida

When I think about my experiences on this course with Mother Divine in Thailand, I think of words like heavenly and bliss and unbounded. They used to be really nice words to say; now I feel I've really experienced all of those on this course. It's a place where everyone should come. It's just beautiful, everything about it.

L.W.—Australia

I learned TM two years ago and I found this as a great help in my life since. TM has become for me my best friend— my oasis where I escape twice a day to let my mind clear and relax. It is like a detox for my mind and offers a sense of security and makes me feel part of the universe. I am gaining more energy, and feel better, stronger, and much happier.

M.W.—Florida

Recently I was on a course at the Mother Divine Program course facility in Thailand. While there I experienced on a very deep, deep level a feeling of care and self-care, but it's not selfish. It just comes up from the bliss, and then you're nourished in your self and then that spills over to everyone else so there's an exchange of being nourished and nourishing, and I see it in all the ladies on my course.

I feel I'll be able to take this into my life. I'll be able to recognize it in people when I see their heart flowing, and then I'll be able to share my heart, and nourish people in that way and nourish myself—and remember to stay connected with the Self and be nourished in that way. That's the source.

A.F.—California

19

WORLD PEACE

"When we enliven the unified field in one place, we enliven it everywhere. It is that field of infinite correlation, where everything is connected with everything else.... This is how we can nourish the minds and hearts of all people around the world."[1]

—Maharishi

O n September 11, 2001 I was peacefully nestled high up in the Blue Ridge Mountains in Boone, North Carolina, completely unaware of what was going on in New York City. At around 12:30 p.m., I turned on the radio, but the music station had been preempted by a special broadcast. At first I was disoriented, as I found it difficult to process what I was hearing in the news. My heart started pounding, and like all Americans, I could not believe that terrorists had crashed into the Twin Towers at the World Trade Center in New York City and the Pentagon in Washington, D.C. I felt a chill of fear run through me at the thought of what could potentially still happen.

Many thoughts ran through my mind. Why would terrorists want to attack the U.S. and hurt innocent people? How could the biggest superpower in the world not foresee or prevent such an attack from a handful of terrorists? The attack revealed to everyone that even after spending over 300 billion dollars on defense per year, our country was completely vulnerable to mass destruction, anywhere, anytime. After enjoying a decade free from the ongoing fear generated by the Cold War, suddenly everything changed. War with an elusive enemy quickly followed.

War has been with us on and off for centuries. World peace has been a long-sought dream of humankind from time immemorial. Is there a way in this day-and-age to really prevent war and enjoy permanent peace on a global scale? After the League of Nations failed to stop the Second World War, the United Nations was established in 1945 to put a final end to conflict between nations. Since its inception, there have been over 186 wars—many with devastating consequences. The miserable failure of the United Nations as a peacekeeping force in the world has simply highlighted the fact that negotiations, sanctions, and even war itself are not an effective means to create lasting peace. In modern recorded history, peace treaties drafted to end or prevent war survive an average of nine years.

In a historic and very insightful speech given on the battleship *Missouri* on September 2, 1945, just after the Japanese surrender, General MacArthur said:

> Military alliances, balances of power, the League of Nations, all in turn have failed. We have had our last chance. The problem basically is theological and involves a spiritual recrudescence [return] and improvement of human character with our almost matchless advance in science.[2]

No one ever really wins in war. The inevitable deaths and untold suffering that result from war cast a deep shadow on any sense of victory that may be gained upon "winning" a war. U.S. President Dwight Eisenhower remarked, "No one has yet explained how war prevents war."[3] President Franklin D. Roosevelt declared, "More than an end to war, we want an end to the beginnings of all wars."[4]

Civil rights activist, Dr. Martin Luther King Jr., said:

> The ultimate weakness of violence is that
> it is a descending spiral,
> begetting the very thing it seeks to destroy.
> Instead of diminishing evil,
> it multiplies it.
> Through violence you may murder the liar,
> but you cannot murder the lie, nor establish the truth.
> Through violence you murder the hater,
> but you do not murder hate.
> In fact, violence merely increases hate....
> Returning violence for violence multiplies violence,
> adding deeper darkness to a night already devoid of stars.
> Darkness cannot drive out darkness;
> Only light can do that.
> Hate cannot drive out hate: only love can do that.[5]

All wars begin with the social tension and stress that fuel fear, misunderstanding, and hostility among factions, religions, and nations. This societal stress and disorder—the chaos in the collective consciousness of any given nation—eventually break out as violent crime, terrorism, or war.

Many religious traditions view killing as a sin. When we kill someone, we are destroying the living expression of transcendental divine bliss consciousness that lies within every human being. What a waste of precious, sacred life!

A radically new approach is needed to stop war. We need a completely new seed if we want to yield a new crop; we need our military academies to focus on and be trained in strategies for creating peace rather than solely on strategies for winning wars.

Heyam dukham anagatam (Yoga Sutra 2:16) is a phrase from the Vedic literature that Maharishi often cited. It means, "Avert the danger before it arises." We need to learn how to prevent the birth of an enemy—to create peace from the level of peace and enliven coherence and harmony in society. We must implement the tools that can help bring peace in every land. One crucial tool is education that enables all to live a creative, happy, successful, and stress-free life, thus eliminating the stress that is the root of poverty, social tension, and collective discontent. In addition, we need to address all the interconnected underlying causes that lead to discontent in a nation, such as poverty, global climate change, ill-health, etc.

When we are no longer bogged down by our own stress and strain, our awareness naturally expands, rather than staying limited to narrow self-interests. As we grow in higher states of consciousness, we start to think of the well-being of our environment. We begin to appreciate the world as our extended family and also gain the clarity necessary to perceive more holistic solutions to critical situations.

As a world family, we are poised on a razor's edge. Climate change is already displaying its first round of effects as devastating hurricanes, forest fires, floods, and strange weather patterns, with the threat of far greater disastrous consequences to come. Terrorism is an ever-present threat. Poverty is widespread in almost all nations, developing and developed alike. The economy is extremely fragile; health-care costs are skyrocketing out of control. In the U.S. alone, over a hundred million people suffer from chronic disease. All these problems add to the stress in the nation, yet our world leaders are curiously slow in their response to these critical situations. They continue blindly driving down the same road as past generations, failing to solve the root cause of these problems.

Although we are living at a very precarious point in time, some interesting underlying events signal a reverse in these negative trends and bring hope that more life-supporting trends are growing in world consciousness. The most exciting positive trend is the significant reduction of violence taking place worldwide.

Canadian evolutionary psychologist Steven Pinker outlines this trend in his new book *The Better Angels of Our Nature: Why Violence has Declined.* His data on violence and war from the past 15,000 years reveals that in prehistoric and pre-modern times the odds of dying from violence averaged around 15%—that is, more than one in six deaths were violent. In modern times, this figure was around 3% worldwide in the 20th century (including all wars, genocides and famines); today it is only about .003%. Pinker outlines many reasons for this dramatic decline, which can together be summed up as: violence no longer makes sense. In the United States, the homicide rate has fallen 50% between 1991 and 2010, and overall crime is at its lowest level in 50 years. According to the FBI's own statistics, crime has significantly decreased across all major areas and in major cities,[6] particularly in the last several years, despite an economic recession when crime usually escalates.

Another example of a positive trend and growing unity in world consciousness is seen in the use of the Internet. The whole Internet revolution is changing the world in dramatic ways. Someone jokingly said to me once, "Google is like God—ask and you shall receive." We can get information about anything immediately. The Internet is a global presence. In an instant, we can be connected to our friends and to events anywhere in the world. We can dramatically change collective consciousness by using the Internet to convey knowledge around the world in a flash. We can have worldwide grassroots campaigns, which are already occurring, to help solve many of the problems we currently face.

We can never have true peace in the world if millions of people are suffering from disease. Thus, to tackle the problem of world peace, we also have to solve the problems of ill health. Governments are lagging behind in fulfilling the desire of communities around the world who want a true health-care system, rather than the "disease care" system we presently have. Health care today is primarily focused on masking or, at best, temporarily relieving the symptoms of disease.

There is a growing awareness that most diseases can be prevented and a corresponding growing interest in holistic medicine—treating the mind and body as a whole rather than just focusing on isolated parts. Sixty percent of Americans are opting to use alternative medicine, fearing the harmful side effects of allopathic medicine and finding its treatment modalities unsuccessful in many cases. There is a growing recognition that drugs only suppress the symptoms of disease and do not address the problem at its source. It is imperative that the health departments of every government change their approach, incorporating health care that inspires the body's own intelligence to defend itself from potential illness and utilizes natural, side-effect-free medicines to resolve existing health problems.

Another movement that is rapidly gaining ground—no pun intended—is organic, sustainable agriculture, which offers a holistic approach to our food system and also has important positive repercussions for health, the economy, and the reversal of poverty.

Eating fresh, organic food is such a simple, commonsense way to prevent future problems such as heart disease, cancer, and obesity. Even Walmart is starting to carry organic foods. So why doesn't organic completely replace "conventional" foods? Because the U.S. government gives huge subsidies to the agro-chemical industry and, in comparison, gives very little support to the organic food industry. This is why fast foods are still artificially cheap and organic food is more expensive.

Fortunately, there is a growing demand for organic food. The First Lady, Michelle Obama, organized the planting of an organic vegetable garden on the White House lawn. She has also taken on the task of dispelling the alarming epidemic of obesity in this generation and continually speaks out about the importance of eating right to stay healthy. The well-known English chef, Jamie Oliver, successfully initiated a change for better nutrition in England's public schools; he also undertook a similar project in the most statistically unhealthy community in America—Huntington, West Virginia. When watching his reality TV show, I was shocked to see what the children in the school there were eating—frozen pizza for breakfast, frozen French fries and processed chicken for lunch, no fresh fruits or vegetables.

Jamie Oliver went to one of the school's classes with a variety of fresh vegetables, and not one child could identify any of them. These kids have rarely ever used forks or knives, as they have grown up on fast food. In seeing this, I was reeling inside in disbelief. This is what our government supports, and we wonder why we have a health-care crisis? It is utter insanity!

A recent article in the *Huffington Post* stated that a new analysis of U.S. health data links children's attention-deficit disorder with exposure to common pesticides used on fruits and vegetables.[7] While the study couldn't prove that pesticides used in agriculture contribute to childhood learning problems, experts said the research is persuasive. Margaret Reeves, senior scientist with the Pesticide Action Network, an advocacy group focused on ending the use of many pesticides, said that the study provides more evidence that the government should encourage farmers to switch to organic methods.

Another sign of awakening in world consciousness is the blossoming of a "global green revolution." New technologies in areas such as clean, sustainable energy are being developed and refined every day. Technologies that allow us to build carbon-neutral buildings, and even entire cities, already exist. If used on a large scale, these can eliminate a substantial percentage of the greenhouse gases that are a major contributing factor to global climate change.

For decades, technologies have been made available that increase fuel efficiency in motor vehicles to an astounding 80 miles per gallon. Why have these technologies not been widely implemented? For the simple reason that powerful lobbies from industries, such as the oil industry, control government policies through enormous financial contributions, to perpetuate government subsidies on oil and other polluting, outdated technologies.

In 2011, the first plug-in electric vehicles hit the road in the United States. The Chevy Volt and Nissan Leaf will hopefully initiate a massive switch to clean, sustainable automotive energy. The popularity of hybrids like the Prius already signals a big awakening in collective awareness and a willingness on the part of many Americans to adopt a more sustainable lifestyle. In Europe, public awareness of serious global environmental concerns is even greater, and governmental support for green technologies there far surpasses that of the United States.

The "organic revolution" underway includes not only organic food, but also natural, non-toxic products for a completely healthy environment and lifestyle. These products range from eco-furniture and building materials to natural household products, organic clothing and bedding, and organic skin and body care.

A growing concern in public health today is the so-called "Sick Building Syndrome." Scientists are finding that where you live and work can literally make you sick! We are exposed to over 60,000 chemicals daily in our environment from toxic building materials and furniture, household cleaning products, and pollutants in the air. As people become more aware of the damaging effects of chemicals on themselves and on the environment, there is a growing demand for all things organic and eco-friendly.

There are many forces that shape our world: political, economic, environmental, cultural, etc. Is there an underlying, unseen phenomenon or force quietly triggering this awakening of humanity towards more positive trends?

In the late 1950s, when Maharishi began his first world tour to teach Transcendental Meditation everywhere, he predicted that if one percent of the population in any society—a city or even a nation—practiced Transcendental Meditation, negative trends in that society would automatically decrease and positive trends would rise. After many studies verified Maharishi's words, scientists named this phenomenon the Maharishi Effect in honor of Maharishi's prediction and his technology of Transcendental Meditation that produced the effect [see Chapter 8].

In 1976, when Maharishi introduced the Transcendental Meditation Sidhi Program, including Yogic Flying, he envisioned that through this powerful technology, which trains human awareness to think and act from the source of all the laws of nature, just the square root of one percent of the population practicing this technology of consciousness in a group would create the same dramatic reversal of negative to positive trends in society. Utilizing this extended Maharishi Effect to its fullest, with a large enough group—the square root of one percent of the world's population, which is currently approximately 8,000 people—world peace can be achieved from one place on earth.

To date there have been almost 50 scientific research studies on the extended Maharishi Effect, many of which have been published in leading scientific journals, such as *Journal of Conflict Resolution, Social Indicators Research, Psychology and the Law, Journal of Offender Rehabilitation, Journal of Social Behavior and Personality, and The Journal of Mind and Behavior.* These studies repeatedly confirm this phenomenon of growing positive tendencies and falling negative trends whenever the square root of one percent of a population have come together to practice the Transcendental Meditation Sidhi Program including Yogic Flying.[8]

Even with the wealth of scientific research corroborating the Maharishi Effect, people have a hard time understanding how groups of people practicing the Transcendental Meditation Sidhi Program can create this powerful effect of coherence and peace in the world. This concept may be easier to grasp with a few examples.

Have you ever driven by a prison? If so, you probably noticed the tension hanging like a thick dark cloud in the air. In my first year of college in England, I took a criminology course and, as part of the course, I visited a rehabilitation prison in Buckinghamshire called Grendon Underwood. The prison was not even maximum security.

When I left the prison and came home that afternoon, I had a horrific headache and felt totally dragged down. I wanted to take a hot bath immediately to wash off the stressed-out feeling. I even threw out the clothes I was wearing that day because it felt like the stress from the prison had penetrated into them.

I am sure you have had the experience of walking into a room when two people are arguing. Again, you can immediately feel the tension in the air. In contrast, if you approach a country church, you experience the opposite. You feel calmed by the delicate sounds of birds singing, and soothed by the soft wind blowing on your face. If you walk into the church, you can't help but feel the stillness inside. When you leave, you feel refreshed and renewed by the peaceful atmosphere.

Every thought, speech, and action is a vibration that spills into the atmosphere. Strong negative vibrations, like the tension in a prison or war zone, are impossible to miss. Of course, there are different levels of tension, covering the full gamut of human emotions from minor annoyances to intense anxiety and violence.

Peaceful vibrations may be more subtle, but they have an equally or even more powerful influence on the environment. For this reason, they are able to neutralize negativity. One type of peaceful vibrations, such as those produced by positive thinking and prayer, remains more or less on the surface level and has a limited effect. However, the deepest, most powerful level of peace, which is the state of pure, absolute stillness—transcendental consciousness—produces an influence at the very basis of existence, the unified field of natural law, which pervades everything. A peaceful influence at this level spreads throughout the world and creates a positive harmonious effect everywhere.

Research on those practicing the Yogic Flying aspect of the Transcendental Meditation Sidhi Program shows that maximum brainwave coherence takes place at the point when the body lifts off the ground.[9] A large group of people enlivening this level of coherence and peace within themselves spontaneously radiates a powerful influence of peace and coherence into the environment.

A Sanskrit verse from the Yoga Sutras (2.35) verifies this principle: *Tat sannidhau vairatyagah,* "In the vicinity of coherence—yoga—hostile tendencies are eliminated."

To date, over five million individuals have learned Transcendental Meditation around the world. There are also large groups of professional "coherence creators"—practitioners of the Transcendental Meditation Sidhi Program including Yogic

Flying—such as a large group at Maharishi University of Management in Fairfield, Iowa. There are also large groups in Europe and South America. In India, a group of 2,000 Vedic Pandits practice Yogic Flying twice daily, and there is an initiative underway[10] to increase this number to over 8,000 in order to generate an influence of coherence for the whole world from one place.

In recent years, over 100,000 students in India and more than 100,000 in South America have begun the practice of Transcendental Meditation and enjoy it as a regular part of their daily curriculum. As this book goes to press, several Latin American governments are introducing Transcendental Meditation into the entire school system in their countries.

Many other schools around the world are adopting this remarkable program, and many hundreds of students in these schools are also being instructed in the Transcendental Meditation Sidhi Program including the Yogic Flying technique.

Maharishi always felt that the military should be the peacekeepers of the nation, not through war, but by preventing the birth of an enemy. By introducing Transcendental Meditation into the armed forces, the military can create a strong effect of coherence and peace in the nation, influencing the government to adopt a peaceful foreign policy and creating an invisible protective shield of coherence for the country. In several countries, the military is now starting to offer Transcendental Meditation and the Transcendental Meditation Sidhi Program to its personnel. This will transform the military from agents of destruction to builders of peace for the nation and the world. In addition, it will save the nation billions of dollars in defense costs—a "win-win" situation for all.

Every time you transcend, you are contributing to peace in the world as a byproduct of your own growing enlightenment. Peace from the level of peace is quietly transforming the world, as all the negative trends prevalent in the world are being replaced by the underlying positive trends now beginning to surface. The large groups of Yogic Flyers in many countries, along with the introduction of Transcendental Meditation and the Transcendental Meditation Sidhi Program into the military and schools around the world, carry the promise that permanent world peace is within our reach!

Power of Peace

What is that power that destroys,
bestowing supremacy?
Every nation's racing to employ
this greatest of fallacies.

What is that power where might is right
declaring victory?
What is this power while death cries in the night
throughout our history?

What is that power of knowledge incomplete,
creating dangerous rivalry,
instilling fear and endless defeat
by ignoring nature's totality?

What is that power where life is suppressed
with every nation in "courageous" conquest?
This is the power of the powerless,
creating a world of peaceless unrest.

What is that power which continually creates
from within the unmanifest—
a dynamic field that silently generates
coherence in world consciousness?

What is that power where right is might,
giving every nation sovereignty?
It's the power of knowledge, life's pure light,
revealed in nature's unity.

This is that power of invincibility
which every nation can gloriously own.
It's the power of harmony amidst diversity—
the laws of nature's home;

Power that prevents the birth of an enemy
is the power of the truly powerful
whose strength lies in unity
for real power is always peaceful.

Experiences

I have been practicing the TM technique all of my adult life. The result of this simple and enjoyable technique over that time is a deep foundation of inner peace and happiness I enjoy each day, no matter what goes on around me. The stability of this contentment allows me to walk through all that life offers and not be overwhelmed by it—good or bad. It is an experience of freedom and wisdom at the same time, a connection with the inner peace and outer happenings of life. I feel gratitude for the stability and happiness that does not sway in the wind, allowing me to enjoy life in fullness.

K.C.—Connecticut

While practicing Yogic Flying I was aware of all the softness in my consciousness, boundaries gently dissolving, softness spreading through the physiology and I could feel wherever my attention flowed outside of myself, the softness flowed into that thing, nurturing it.

P.O.—England

After practicing Transcendental Meditation for some time I now feel more invincible. The first stage of this is that I feel more comfortable to witness conflicting desires, and let them resolve internally. The outcome is a feeling of conflicting desires becoming unified and harmonized into something abstract but somehow rich with qualities, infinitely nourishing, and intimately part of me. It feels like armor. I have a feeling of invincibility, and I feel I am able to face anything.

W.G.—England

In my heart I perceive a circular motion, which is a self-sustaining flow of bliss. This motion seems to dip into the unmanifest and come out again into the manifest in a perpetual circular flow with infinite speed. It reminds me of the term infinite feedback loop. When I come out of meditation little things bring deep waves of bliss, and I feel as if I am acting within a cozy, safe cocoon of infinity.

H.S.—Canada

20

HEAVEN ON EARTH

*"Through the window of science we see the
Dawn of the Age of Enlightenment."*[1]

— Maharishi

In 1991 I went to East Hampton, Long Island, for my grandmother's 90th birthday celebration. The party was attended by about 150 of her family and friends. The following night, I had dinner with about ten family members and close family friends who had attended the celebration.

I was seated next to my cousin's cousin's husband, no relation to me. He had recently retired from being one of Washington D.C.'s most prominent political reporters. In addition to being exceptionally brilliant, extremely opinionated, and a walking encyclopedia of news events, he was, and I hope still is, a very open person who enjoys listening to new ideas. He asked me about my life, and I told him about Transcendental Meditation and Maharishi's goals for the world. At the end of our conversation he said to me, "I applaud what you are doing, I admire your enthusiasm, but the world out there is a cynical place." He probably summed me up as a naive, wide-eyed optimist!

Over the next few days, the Soviet Union collapsed. This event was a dramatic change in world consciousness, freeing the world from the fear that the decades-old Cold War would explode in nuclear conflict. Almost exactly ten years later came the shocking events of 9/11. In an instant, ripples of horror and fear spread around the world. Since then the U.S. has been enmeshed in two wars, in Iraq and Afghanistan. Both the United States and Europe have been struggling to avoid an economic meltdown and, as I am writing this chapter, the Gulf of Mexico is being polluted by millions of barrels of oil every day. In between all this, there was the tragic event of the huge tsunami in Indonesia in 2004, the wonderful city of

New Orleans was nearly wiped out due to Hurricane Katrina in 2005, two devastating earthquakes hit Haiti and Chile in 2010, and another earthquake off the coast of Japan in 2011 caused a tsunami resulting in massive destruction.

On the surface, I think my relative's husband was right. The world at the moment is crippled with fear, cynicism, and greed. Terrorism is a frightening reality that could strike at any moment. Economic and corporate greed is taking precedence over the health and well-being of the citizens in many countries; due to shortsightedness and avarice, many governments and their citizens are unwilling to make the changes necessary to halt climate change, even when faced with increasingly catastrophic natural disasters around the world.

By now you are probably wondering, why did she entitle this chapter "Heaven on Earth?"

Take a look back at the previous chapter on world peace. There are already rays of light on the horizon. "...the first ray of the dawning sun is good enough to dispel the darkness of the night,"[2] said Maharishi.

How will those rays of light become the full sunshine? Will there be a dramatic event that catalyzes a permanent shift in world consciousness? Or will this shift slowly creep upon us, gently casting its soft light like the dawning of a new day? Only time will tell, but one thing is clear: we are on the verge of drowning, and something must happen soon to pull us out of the troubled waters in which we are swimming.

The surface level of life does not always tell the underlying story. In the last chapter, I described many quiet, deeper forces that are gaining strength.

The greatest, yet most underutilized, resource of any nation is its people. It is common knowledge that most people currently use only 10 to 20 percent of their full mental potential. If you think of almost seven billion people in the world using only 20 percent of their brain potential, that means eighty percent of the world's mental capacity is dormant, which is a waste of the most highly sophisticated and powerful machines on this planet! All the problems we are facing today are man-made—a natural result of only using a golf-ball size portion of our brains.

There was a recent broadcast on *60 Minutes*—a popular national TV show—that highlighted the new trend on college campuses of students taking ADHD drugs such as Adderall and Ritalin to boost their academic performance.[3] Many students illegally take these drugs, which help them to stay up all night to cram for exams or get a paper done. These drugs are addictive amphetamines and are debilitating to health. Worse, the long-term side effects are not known. We do know, however, that sleep deprivation is unhealthy for the body and negatively impacts levels of thyroid and stress hormones, which in turn can affect memory, the immune system, the heart, metabolism, and much more—including increasing the risk of cancer. Using these addictive stimulants for studying is an unwise—potentially even very harmful—path for our precious youth to be walking upon.

Instead of allowing our students to damage their health and minds in this way, we should enable them to develop their full mental potential so they naturally are capable of high academic achievement and much more.

Education that develops the full potential of the student is the key to quickly transform the world from an age of ignorance and problems, where people are caught up in small values of life, to an age of enlightenment where everyone is living his or her full potential and enjoying life to the maximum.

Fortunately, beneath the irrational behavior that is seen in colleges, governments, and business, there are people around the world who are beginning to experience a tangible, concrete, scientifically verifiable awakening of their own consciousness. The introduction of the Transcendental Meditation program in educational institutions is creating a new generation of students with more developed minds and orderly thinking, who will be able to contribute to the solutions we desperately need.

A great hero and humanitarian in this area is filmmaker David Lynch, who has raised millions of dollars through the David Lynch Foundation for Consciousness-Based Education and World Peace[4] to teach Transcendental Meditation and the Transcendental Meditation Sidhi Program to hundreds of thousands of students all over the world. Every school in which the Transcendental Meditation program has been implemented has seen dramatic improvements.

In addition to bringing the Transcendental Meditation technique to the world, Maharishi developed an integrative interdisciplinary curriculum, Consciousness-Based Education[SM], for any school to implement. The hallmark of this approach to education is development of the full potential of every student. One of its unique factors involves connecting each part of every discipline the student studies to the wholeness of knowledge and to the student himself, making all knowledge truly practical and relevant.

Many Consciousness-Based[SM] schools that have been established have an open admissions policy. Every student is welcome, regardless of educational and socio-economic background or previous academic performance, and virtually all soon rise to a high level of academic achievement and blossom in their own unique talents.

The Maharishi School of the Age of Enlightenment in Fairfield, Iowa,[5] at which all students and faculty practice Transcendental Meditation, was the first Consciousness-Based school in the United States. It has been in existence for about thirty years now and has an impressive record of excellence:

- Classes consistently score in the top one percent of the nation on standardized tests.

- More than 95% of graduates are accepted at four-year colleges.

- Students receive top international, national, and state awards in science, mathematics, art, theater, photography, poetry, and writing.

- Students have won more top-ten finishes at the global finals of creative problem-solving competitions than any other school in the world.

- Students exhibit extraordinary athletic successes, including 17 state tennis championships in the past 15 years.

Many humanitarians are recognizing the importance of education to solve the problem of war. Greg Mortenson, known as the "gentle giant" and author of the *New York Times* bestseller *Three Cups of Tea*, has established over 100 schools in villages in Pakistan and Afghanistan. He feels the approach of educating children, especially girls, is a much more effective way of solving the problem of terrorism than the ill-fated approach of war. Colin Powell, Barbara and Laura Bush, John Kerry, and many top generals have read his book; *Three Cups of Tea* is now required reading at the Pentagon.

There is a popular African saying that states, "If you educate a man, you educate an individual, but if you educate a girl, you educate a whole community." The minds of young girls are a severely underutilized resource in developing nations, and making education available to them will create a powerful force of creativity and intelligence soon to be reckoned with in a welcoming way!

The students around the world practicing the Transcendental Meditation technique in their schools are generators of coherence and peace from within. Maharishi often said that the power of right—the power of knowledge—is much stronger than the power of might, and that establishing peace through education is the first step in creating heaven on earth.

The second step is to eradicate poverty. As Maharishi has explained, poverty is a major cause of terrorism and conflict. Maharishi has formulated programs to eradicate poverty through developing unused, uncontaminated lands around the world to grow organic produce. Each community that starts an agricultural project will also have a Consciousness-Based school for children, incorporating the Transcendental Meditation program. This will ensure that the problems of both poverty and education are tackled at the same time.

Fortunately, world thinkers are also beginning to recognize the link between peace and the eradication of poverty, as shown by the fact that in 2006, the Nobel Peace prize was awarded to Muhammad Yunus for his pioneering efforts to create economic and social development through microfinancing.

There are many visionaries and heads of foundations that are thinking very big and developing many successful approaches to solving the problems of poverty. In addition to microfinancing, these innovations include "patient capital" philanthropy and socially responsible business models. These individuals and organizations are forming partnerships and sharing experiences of solutions that have been found to be most effective.

Paul Hawken, author of the book *Blessed Unrest*,[6] has described all these groups as comprising the world's largest "movement," which is made up of millions of organizations worldwide working to improve the quality of life in their areas and internationally. The organizations are mostly connected around the themes of social justice, environmental sustainability, and preservation of indigenous cultures.

There are many more innovations that are works in progress to solve the myriad problems in the world. I recently received an email containing an unusual idea in an article entitled, "Plastic Paradise":

An island the size of Hawaii made entirely from plastic bottles could become the hottest postcode on earth and is part of an incredible environmental vision for the future. CGI images show how a team of Dutch scientists plans to take 44 million kilos of plastic waste currently bobbing around in the Pacific Ocean and transform it into Recycled Island. Solar and wave energy will be used to sustain the island and its 500,000 inhabitants.[7]

Over 300 million people have watched TED (Technology, Entertainment, and Design) Talks, which are available online and feature inspiring designers, musicians, and thought leaders, many of whom offer creative solutions to the world's challenges. These talks are even being viewed in remote areas of the world, often inspiring TEDx local conferences that highlight the top thinkers and artists in those communities. This venue allows for the free exchange of effective ideas all around the world simply through the Internet.

In addition to all these innovations being developed, philanthropists are coming forward to support these solutions. Through the Giving Pledge, Warren Buffet and Bill Gates are asking all billionaires to give half of their wealth to philanthropy before their death to help fund viable solutions to the pressing problems we face today.[8] Many of these billionaires don't want to give their money blindly—they also want to be involved in the projects to make sure they are successful. They are joining forces with each other and with governments to formulate effective approaches to the major world crises. These entrepreneurs who have been so successful in business will most likely also be effective at implementing solutions.

Many countries are drowning in debt due to the increasing costs of health care, war, cleaning up environmental disasters, etc. Think of the billions of dollars we could be saving by investing in prevention, which would reduce health-care, military, prison, and environmental costs. We could then use that money to build more schools, better roads and transportation systems, and better housing for those who really need it.

The problems in the world today are complex, but the solutions are simple. Is it really so naive to think that the world can wake up and realize that:

- Eating pure organic food is a far better means of creating health than the consumption of highly processed, genetically modified, pesticide-ridden food;
- Preventing disease is a vastly better approach to creating good health than treating the symptoms of disease with medication, which in many cases has terrible side effects, often as bad as the disease itself;
- Eradicating poverty, through such programs as microfinancing to help the poor pull themselves out of poverty, is more effective than giving money to corrupt or ineffective governments, who continuously fail to raise their nations above poverty and are moreover held hostage by the debt they have

accumulated;

- Developing energy self-sufficiency is greatly preferable and the prerequisite for economic self-sufficiency rather than dependence on other nations for energy needs;
- Creating peace from the level of peace to calm tensions in the world is obviously better than trying to create peace through war, which only generates hate, anger, and sorrow;

And most importantly:

- Developing the full creative potential of the citizens of the nation, as the basis to prevent crime, terrorism, and ill-health and bring innovative solutions to the nation, is the most practical and effective way to go.

As we have already discussed in previous chapters, Maharishi developed programs to bring fulfillment to absolutely every area of society, from education to agriculture, from national defense to health care. There is more than enough scientific research verifying the positive benefits of each of these programs.

As more unity and coherence rise in world consciousness due to the large groups of students all over the world practicing Transcendental Meditation and the Transcendental Meditation Sidhi Program, people will appreciate the creative ideas that can address our global challenges and will focus their attention on implementing them. Governments will spontaneously change to meet the demands of their citizens for a peaceful, healthy, better world.

There are hundreds of thousands of people who are enjoying heaven on earth right now in their own lives as a result of their practice of Transcendental Meditation and the Transcendental Meditation Sidhi Program. I am sure these individuals want the whole world to enjoy this reality, because they are experiencing it in their own lives, and it is only natural to want to share something good.

Change begins within; peace begins within; heaven begins within. Just as a tiny wave can rise into a powerful tidal wave, the gentle, coherent ripple of one person meditating, merging with the ripples of millions of other people around the world also meditating, will create that tidal wave that will change the destiny of the world into the dawning sunshine of heaven on earth. As Maharishi said:

Heaven on earth on the *individual* level will be characterized by perfect health, long life in bliss, the ability to effortlessly fulfill one's desires, and living always in a beautiful, ever-fresh and nourishing environment. Heaven on earth on the *collective* level will be characterized by indomitable positivity, harmony, and peace on all levels of collective life—family, community, nation, and the world.[9]

Every day I feel so deeply blessed for the heaven I am experiencing in my life and feel so grateful to be alive to observe the changing time that is unfolding before my eyes.

There is something so inexpressibly captivating about waking up in the morning to enjoy a golden sunrise, the brilliance of the first sparkling rays, and the melodious sound of the morning birds. I am enjoying seeing the first delicate rays of a new time in all the tender young children who are experiencing the heavenly light of their own pure consciousness through their practice of the Transcendental Meditation technique. I look forward to seeing this dawn rise to the full sunshine of heaven on earth.

My Heaven

If I could create my own heaven,
how would I like it to be?
I'd make it just as it is now–
the heaven that exists inside me.

It's a perfect place of pure silence
that percolates in bubbling bliss,
then opens into soothing waves—
the sea rising, then falling in stillness.

My heaven shimmers with light
humming within me as silence's song,
and blissfully pulsates in my physiology
lighting each cell like the golden dawn.

Rivers of nectar flow from my heart,
I delight in its sumptuous taste.
It is purest love that exists
in which all life is interlaced.

Tendrils of my feelings extend to infinity
embracing the entire universe
and pour to God in deepest gratitude
for this gift—my beloved Heaven on Earth.

Experiences

I feel amazing during meditation, so relaxed, like nothing can touch me, like I'm up on a cloud. It's perfect. And for just twenty minutes of my time I'm getting so much more, so much rest and I really enjoy it. I think the world would be an amazing place if everybody had this.

E.M.—New York

At times during my practice of the TM program and its advanced techniques I feel a gentle swelling from deep inside my awareness and a sense of huge expansion. The softness and depth of the experience feels so sublime that a thought of heaven naturally comes, and a feeling of thank you for all the blessings that we have been given in this life here on earth. After such an experience wells up, my senses are totally heightened.   Colors, textures, food, sounds—everything has a fullness that brings waves of happiness and contentment to my heart.

L.G.—New York

One morning what woke me up were the golden pulsations of bubbling bliss percolating throughout my physiology. It was so delightful. As I got ready to go out for my morning walk in the nearby woods, my inner bliss didn't dissipate, but rather increased. Then it started pouring through my senses. I could taste it, feel it, touch it, and see it. It was lively not just inside but outside as well, in everything—in every branch, the tender chirp of every bird, and in the air itself. I began to recognize that the bliss outside of me was the same as the bliss in my physiology and both started to swell even more. I was just a body of bliss walking through bliss and even though I could perceive the values of nature's diversity—the trees, the sky, and the sun streaming through everything—I felt it was all me. It was a taste of what life could and should be—Heaven on Earth.

M.K.—Missouri

CONCLUSION

I have been practicing Transcendental Meditation for over 38 years. I have only missed a meditation on the rarest of occasions. My regular practice of meditation has nothing to do with discipline, but everything to do with deeply enjoying the experience and the clarity and lightness I feel after I meditate.

My life has not always been smooth sailing, and I have definitely had to navigate some rough seas. The first major storm I hit was about six months after I had learned Transcendental Meditation, when my father unexpectedly passed away at age 51 from a heart attack. This was a huge shock to my family.

My father enjoyed life and people more than anyone I have ever met. I was very close to him, and we used to have lively debates on many topics such as education, politics, religion, and philosophy. My father always stood up for what he believed in, and it was a great source of satisfaction for me when he questioned my ideas and I could meet his challenges. I always thought his challenges were his way of teaching me to stand up for what I believed in.

I still miss him and wish he were here today to see the unexpected direction my life took. When he died, I felt I had been deeply stung in my heart, but every time I meditated, I felt an incredible wave of soothing peace overtake my whole being. For about a year after he passed away, I had a nagging pain inside and my heart felt blocked. I could directly feel that each time I meditated, the pain became less and less, and soon it subsided. I felt so lucky to have had a way to release the sorrow I was feeling, rather than burying the pain and anger I felt when my father died, only to have it surface at some later point in my life. In time, I felt freer inside and more at peace about the whole thing. The tremendous calmness and strength I derived from my meditations during this delicate time really cemented my belief in the value of my practice of Transcendental Meditation.

I have also faced the challenges that everyone has in work situations—managing workloads, pressures of deadlines, dealing with different personalities, etc. There have been other trying situations as well, but through them all, meditating has been an anchor to help me maintain my stability and calm in the midst of those occasional rough waters.

Before I started Transcendental Meditation, I viewed life in a linear fashion, appreciating only the superficial values of people and life. After some time of meditating, I noticed that I was starting to view life more vertically—looking beyond the surface level of people and events. Using the ocean as an analogy, the changing, dancing waves on the surface of the ocean ceased to dominate my vision, and I began to look within the ocean and discover the endless variety of fish inside. I became curious as to what lay at the bottom, and how the different forces and currents within structured the way the waves formed on the surface. This is just a graphic way of saying that as my inner world of unbounded awareness became more clear, stable, and rich, life and people had more charm, meaning, and depth. I became fascinated with everything.

Now, after many years have passed by, I feel I am perceiving life from the inside out: anchored to the bottom of the ocean, I recognize all the waves on the surface as connected to the whole ocean and know that I am the whole ocean—depth, waves, and all.

I also feel largely free from the swings of outside circumstances; I am now the director of my own play. Every person who walks into my play neatly fits into my stage design. I naturally have more control over my life; I feel self-empowered. There are still challenging scenes that pop up now and then that I would prefer to cut from my play, but I see the wholeness of the play now and view it all as a changing, entertaining production, so those unwanted situations don't bother me as they would have in the past. I am more able to stand back and observe difficult situations in an easy and objective way.

There is an underlying contentment and sense of fulfillment in life, and in all my activities. Some days are smoother than others, but on the whole life is always improving. "It's getting better all the time," to borrow a phrase from one of the Beatles' famous songs. Naturally I can't help but wish for everyone in the world to enjoy the benefits of practicing the Transcendental Meditation technique and the Transcendental Meditation Sidhi Program.

It amazes me to know that every person of the over seven billion population in the world can experience the same unbounded bliss inside, no matter what their race, religion, or socio-economic background. This is because every person on earth has the state of pure consciousness within. We can think actively, we can think more quietly, and innate in the ability to think more quietly is the ability for the mind to be completely still. This inner stillness is a universal reality, and it is the one experience in life that is accessible to all, the one experience that can unify the world because it already underlies and permeates the world at its most fundamental level.

Amelia Earhart wanted to fly with the stars. She wanted to live a life without borders, where the horizon was her constant view. She wanted to fly on top of the world. "What do dreams know of boundaries?"[1] Amelia Earhart said. She lived her dreams and broke boundaries that no one else dared to break.

Every individual, without going anywhere, can now fly inside and explore inner space without limits and enjoy the boundless, luminous expanse of bliss that exists at the depth of each one of us. Every person can become the totality of the universe with its thousands of brilliant galaxies and numberless suns, moons, and stars. On this ground of total natural law, everyone can gain the ability to effortlessly fulfill their highest dreams.

I feel I have only touched the surface of the possibilities and profundity that lies inside. I know there is a bottomless well of endless fascination waiting to be explored. It is completely impossible to describe the beauty, bliss, and pure love that exist inside our hearts and minds. I feel incredibly blessed for the unexpected turn my life took when I was 18 years old.

Naturally, I want to express appreciation and gratitude to the tradition of Vedic Masters who have passed this knowledge of totality of life from teacher to teacher, preserving it since time immemorial, and to Maharishi, the representative of this tradition of supreme knowledge in our generation, who worked non-stop for over 50 years to bring this knowledge and these technologies of consciousness to the world.

I believe that Maharishi's vision of heaven on earth will soon be a reality. The first rays of the sun are already dawning in the millions of fortunate souls around the world who are enjoying heaven on earth within through their practice of the Transcendental Meditation technique, and it is just a matter of time before the soft dawn bursts into the bright midday sun.

Let Your Soul Sing

Love comes in many forms.
Purest love appears in the formless;
Unquantified, it is an all-embracing,
Unbounded ocean of love.
Shapeless love bubbles and swirls
Into its divine ecstasy.
Impersonal, it unconditionally loves
Everyone and everything.
Unseen like the soft wind
It shines like the golden sun;
Soundless, it is the eternal music
Of your soul singing.

NOTES

Chapter 1: Coming Home

1. Maharishi Mahesh Yogi, *Bhagavad Gita: A New Translation and Commentary, Chapters 1-6* (Washington, D.C.: Age of Enlightenment Press, c1967; fifth printing 1984), 313.(6:20)

2. Hafiz, *The Gift: Poems by Hafiz, the Great Sufi Master,* trans. Daniel Ladinsky (New York: Penguin Group, 1999), 19.

Chapter 2: The Inward Journey— Transcendental Consciousness

1. Maharishi Mahesh Yogi, Global Press Conference, August 24, 2005.

2. Maharishi Mahesh Yogi, *His Holiness Maharishi Mahesh Yogi, Thirty Years Around the World—Dawn of the Age of Enlightenment, Volume One 1957-1964* (Netherlands: MVU Press, 1986), 189.

3. Maharishi, *Thirty Years Around the World,* 189.

4. Maharishi, *Thirty Years Around the World,* 190.

5. Emily Dickinson. *The Complete Poems of Emily Dickinson.* Boston: Little, Brown, 1924; Bartleby.com (2000), http://www.bartleby.com/113/5025.html.

6. Henry David Thoreau, *The Journal of Henry D. Thoreau: In Fourteen Volumes Bound as Two: Volumes I-VII (1837- October 1855)* ed. Bradford Torrey and F. H. Allen (New York: Courier Dover Publications, 1962), 31-32.

7. Torrey and Allen, *The Journal of Henry D. Thoreau,* 211.

8. Eugene Ionesco, *Present Past, Past Present,* trans. Helen R. Lane (New York: Grove Press, 1971), 151–154.

9. Dickinson, *The Complete Poems of Emily Dickinson,* http://www. bartleby.com/113/1126.html.

10. Quoted in Michael Murphy and Rhea A. White, *In The Zone: Transcendent Experience in Sports* (New York: Penguin, 1995, rev. ed. of: *The Psychic Side of Sports,* c1978), 11.

11. Quoted in Murphy and White, *In The Zone,* 11.

12. Quoted in Murphy and White, *In The Zone,* 108-109.

13. Quoted in Craig Pearson, "Laozi and the Tao Te Ching: The ancient wisdom of China," http://www.tm.org/blog/medit-ation/laozi-and-the-tao-te-ching-the-ancient-wisdom-of-china/.

Chapter 3: Transformations

1. Maharishi Mahesh Yogi, *Maharishi Speaks to Students: Mastery over Natural Law, Volume 2/4* (India: Age of Enlightenment Publications, 1997), 45.

2. David Lynch, *Catching the Big Fish: Meditation, Consciousness, and Creativity* (New York: Penguin Group, 2006), 27-28.

3. Arthur M. Abell, *Talks with Great Composers* (Philosophical Library, Inc., c1955, 1987; reprint, New York: Carol Publishing Group, 1994), 86.

Chapter 4: Cosmic Consciousness—Being in the Zone

1. Maharishi Mahesh Yogi, *Science of Being and Art of Living* (Age of Enlightenment Publications, c1963; reprint, New York: Meridian, 1995), 80.

2. Quoted in Murphy and White, *In The Zone,* 27.

3. Quoted in Murphy and White, *In The Zone,* 14.

4. Puki Freeberg, "Women College Athletes Train with TM," http://www.tm.org/blog/people/women-college-squash-transc endental-meditation/.

5. R.W. Emerson, "II Self-Reliance," http://www.rwe.org/com plete-works/ii—essays-i/ii-self-reliance.html, paragraph 9.

Chapter 5: God Consciousness

1. Maharishi, *Thirty Years Around the World*, 151.

2. Murphy and White, *In The Zone*, 1.

3. Helen Keller, *My Religion* (New York: The Swedenborg Foundation, c1980; reprint, San Diego: The Book Tree, 2007), 27-28.

Chapter 6: Unity Consciousness

1. Quoted in Craig Pearson, *The Complete Book of Yogic Flying: Maharishi Mahesh Yogi's Program for Enlightenment and Invincibility* (Fairfield, Iowa: Maharishi University of Management Press, 2008), 83.

2. Maharishi, *Science of Being and Art of Living*, xvii.

3. Maharishi, *Bhagavad Gita: A New Translation and Commentary*, 331-332.   (6:31)

4. Quoted in Robert Keith Wallace, *The Neurophysiology of Enlightenment* (Fairfield, Iowa: Maharishi University of Management Press, c1986; fifth printing 1997), 294.

5. R.W. Emerson, "IX The Over-Soul," http://www.rwe.org/com plete/complete-works/ii-essays-i/iv-the-over-soul.html, paragraph 3.

6. William Shatner, "William Shatner!" interview by Tom Ashbrook, http://onpoint.wbur.org/2010/10/07/william-shatner.

Chapter 7: Kingdom of Heaven Within

1. Maharishi, *Thirty Years Around the World*, 165.

Chapter 8: Transcendental Meditation Sidhi Program

1. Maharishi, *Science of Being and Art of Living*, xxi.

2. Vedic means pertaining to Veda. *Veda* is a Sanskrit word that means knowledge—pure knowledge— knowledge of the Self. It is the knowledge of the eternal reality that is present at the unmanifest basis of creation. The Vedic literature is the ancient literature of India, cognized by ancient *rishis*, or seers, in their own consciousness. It has been preserved orally generation after generation, passed from parents to children in the Vedic families of India, but was written down about 3000 B.C. Maharishi always emphasized that the essence of the Veda is found in the universal experience of transcendental consciousness, not in the written texts of the Vedic literature.

3. F.T. Travis and D.W. Orme-Johnson, "EEG Coherence and Power during Yogic Flying," *International Journal of Neuroscience 54* (1990), 1–12.

4. Pearson, *The Complete Book of Yogic Flying*, 64-65, 118-119, 124-125.

5. Pearson, *The Complete Book of Yogic Flying*, 498-506.

6. Pearson, *The Complete Book of Yogic Flying*, 408-409.

7. Robert M. Oates, *Permanent Peace: How to Stop Terrorism and War–Now and Forever* (c1988; revised, Fairfield, Iowa: Institute of Science, Technology, and Public Policy, 2002), 66. (see *Journal of Conflict Resolution, 32*, 776-812)

8. Pearson, *The Complete Book of Yogic Flying*, 548.

9. Pearson, *The Complete Book of Yogic Flying*, 550.

10. Pearson, *The Complete Book of Yogic Flying*, 548, 551.

Chapter 9: Enlightenment, Is It Possible?

1. Robert M. Oates, Jr., *Celebrating the Dawn: Maharishi Mahesh Yogi and the TM Technique* (New York: G. P. Putnam's Sons, 1976), 37.

2. Pearson, *The Complete Book of Yogic Flying*, 39.

3. Quoted in Pearson, *The Complete Book of Yogic Flying*, 39.

4. Pearson, *The Complete Book of Yogic Flying*, 58.

Chapter 10: Neurophysiology of Enlightenment

1. Oates, *Celebrating the Dawn*, 84.

2. Wallace, *The Neurophysiology of Enlightenment*, 57-58.

3. Wallace, *The Neurophysiology of Enlightenment*, 57-58.

4. Quoted in Wallace, *The Neurophysiology of Enlightenment*, 294.

5. Maharishi, *Bhagavad Gita: A New Translation and Commentary*, 124. (2:72)

6. *Scientific Research on the Transcendental Meditation Program: Collected Papers, Vol. 1- 6.* Vlodrop, The Netherlands: MVU Press.

7. Youtube.com, "Norman Rosenthal, M.D. on Transcendental Meditation," http://www.youtube.com/watch?v=10XeslMRbiw.

8. Pearson, *The Complete Book of Yogic Flying*, 90-91.

   See also: F.T. Travis, "Eyes Open and TM EEG Patterns After One and After Eight Years of TM Practice," *Psychophysiology* 28(3a)(1991), S58.

9. Pearson, *The Complete Book of Yogic Flying*, 91.

   See also: F.T. Travis, J. J. Teece, A. Arenander, and R. K. Wallace, "Patterns of EEG Coherence, Power, and Contingent Negative Variation Characterize the Integration of Transcendental and Waking States," *Biological Psychology* 61 (2002), 293-319.

10. Pearson, *The Complete Book of Yogic Flying*, 91.

11. Pearson, *The Complete Book of Yogic Flying*, 77.

12. H. Harung, F. Travis, W. Blank, D. Heaton, "Higher Development, Brain Integration, and Excellence in Leadership," *Management Decision* 47(6)(2009), 872-894.

13. Quoted in Global Good News, "Higher consciousness for higher achievement: Brain integration in world-class performers similar to Transcendental Meditation effects," http://newer.global goodnews.info/science-news-a.html?art=125745313244984571, paragraph 5.

14. *Scientific Research on the Transcendental Meditation Program: Collected Papers, Vol. 1-6.*

15. Pearson, *The Complete Book of Yogic Flying*, 602.

Chapter 11: Bliss

1. Maharishi, *Thirty Years Around the World*, 47.

2. Maharishi, *Thirty Years Around the World*, 97.

3. Quoted in Lynch, *Catching the Big Fish*, 7.

4. Maharishi, *Thirty Years Around the World*, 124.

Chapter 12: In Love

1. Maharishi Mahesh Yogi, *Love and God* (Oslo, Norway: Spiritual Regeneration Movement, 1965), 15.

2. Maharishi, *Love and God*, 19-20.

Chapter 13: The World Is As You Are

1. Maharishi, Global Press Conference, October 12, 2005.

2. Maharishi, *Bhagavad Gita: A New Translation and Commentary*, 292. (6:5)

Chapter 14: The Secret Beyond *The Secret*

1. Quoted in Pearson, *The Complete Book of Yogic Flying*, 159.

2. Quoted in Pearson, *The Complete Book of Yogic Flying*, 136.

3. Quoted in Pearson, *The Complete Book of Yogic Flying*, 136.

4. Quoted in Oates, *Permanent Peace*, 122.

5. Quoted in Pearson, *The Complete Book of Yogic Flying*, 138.

6. *Scientific Research on the Maharishi Transcendental Meditation and TM-Sidhi Programs: A Brief Summary of 500 Studies* (Fairfield, Iowa: Maharishi University of Management Press, 1996), 12-13, 16, 18-19.

7. Maharishi, *Bhagavad Gita: A New Translation and Commentary*, 96-97. (2:48)

Chapter 15: The Music of Your Soul

1. Maharishi University of Management, "Courses for the Creative Musical Arts Program at Maharishi University of Management" [accessed October 27, 2010], http://www.mum.edu/music/courses.html.

2. Music with Ease, "Famous Quotes: Ludwig van Beethoven," [accessed October 1, 2010], http://www.musicwithease.com/beethoven-quotes.html.

3. "Definition of music by the Free Online Dictionary, Thesaurus and Encyclopedia," http://www.thefreedictionary.com/music.

4. Maharishi, *Maharishi Speaks to Students*, 50.

5. Maharishi, *Maharishi Speaks to Students*, 48.

6. Abell, *Talks with Great Composers*, 5-6.

7. Maharishi Gandharva Veda—the Eternal Music of Nature, "Maharishi about Gandharva Veda," http://www.maharishi-gandharva-veda.com/page4.htm, paragraph 7.

8. "Maharishi about Gandharva Veda," paragraph 1.

9. "Maharishi about Gandharva Veda," paragraph 3.

10. Quoted in Murphy and White, *In The Zone*, 33.

11. Aldous Huxley, "Music at Night," 1931. Quoted at http://www. quotationspage.com/quote/1654.html.

12. Ladinsky, *The Gift: Poems by Hafiz*, 16.

13. Wordsworth, William. *The Complete Poetical Works*. London: Macmillan and Co., 1888; Bartleby.com, 1999, "COMPOSED A FEW MILES ABOVE TINTERN ABBEY, ON REVISITING THE BANKS OF THE WYE DURING A TOUR. JULY 13, 1798," http://www.bartleby.com/145/ww138.html, lines 93-101.

14. Ladinsky, *The Gift: Poems by Hafiz*, 3.

15. Thomas Carlyle, *Works*, 5:83–84. Quoted at "The Carlyle Letters Online," http://carlyleletters.dukejournals.org/cgi/content/full/31/1/lt-18560425-TC-RB-01, footnote 3.

16. Maharishi, *Maharishi Speaks to Students*, 50.

17. Maharishi, *Maharishi Speaks to Students*, 50-51.

18. Maharishi, *Maharishi Speaks to Students*, 51.

19. Maharishi, *Maharishi Speaks to Students*, 51.

20. Don Robertson, "The Effect of Music on Plants (The Plant Experiments)" [accessed February 8, 2011], http://www.dove song. com/positive_music/plant_experiments.asp.

21. David Evans, "The effectiveness of music as an intervention for hospital patients: a systematic review," *Journal of Advanced Nursing* 37 (1)(2002), 8–18. http://onlinelibrary.wiley.com/doi/10.1046/j.1365-2648.2002.02052.x/full

22. Quoted in Elliot M. Galkin, *A History of Orchestral Conducting in Theory and Practice* (Pendragon Press, 1988), 735-736.

Chapter 16: Religion, Science, and New Age Spirituality

1. Maharishi, *Science of Being and Art of Living*, 251.

2. Maharishi, *Bhagavad Gita: A New Translation and Commentary*, preface.

3. Maharishi, *Bhagavad Gita: A New Translation and Commentary*, 6.

4. Maharishi, *Thirty Years Around the World*, 334.

5. Bob Roth, "Father Len Dubi: How TM enriches my religious life," http://www.tm.org/blog/people/christianity-and-trans cendental-meditation-father-dubi-interview.

6. The Transcendental Meditation Program, [accessed October 1, 2010], http://www.tm.org/meditation-techniques, section: What religious leaders say.

7. David Lynch Foundation Television, "Saving the Disposable Ones Documentary," http://dlf.tv/2010/disposable-ones.

8. Bob Roth, "Orthodox Rabbi speaks on his 9-year TM practice," http://www.tm.org/blog/people/rabbi-transcendental-meditat ion.
   The Transcendental Meditation Program, section: What religious leaders say.

9. The Transcendental Meditation Program, section: What religious leaders say.

10. Maharishi, *Thirty Years Around the World*, 335.

11. Rachel L. Swarns, "Fergie, Yoga and Green Eggs: The White House Easter Egg Roll," http://thecaucus.blogs.nytimes.com/ 2009/04/13/fergie-yoga-and-green-eggs-the-white-house-easter-egg-roll.

12. Global Good News, "National Meditation Month, USA: Brain research identifies three types of meditation," http://www.glo-balgoodnews.com/science-news-a.html?art=12735292172052243.

See also: F. Travis and J. Shear, "Focused attention, open monitoring and automatic self-transcending: Categories to organize meditations from Vedic, Buddhist and Chinese traditions," *Consciousness and Cognition* 19(4)(2010): 1110-8.

13. Global Good News, "Brain research identifies three types of meditation."

14. Global Good News, "Brain research identifies three types of meditation."

15. Meta-analysis, an objective means of drawing conclusions about an entire field of research, is a good way to compare many different studies, which could individually have positive or negative results. In comprehensive meta-analyses comparing various meditation and stress-reduction techniques, the Transcendental Meditation technique is shown to reduce high blood pressure, anxiety, and substance abuse—results not produced by other techniques. In fact, scientists found that concentration techniques may actually increase anxiety, and some meditation techniques have no more effect than a placebo.

16. Physorg.com, "Transcendental Meditation activates default mode network, the brain's natural ground state," http://www. physorg.com/news186930412.html.

17. The Transcendental Meditation Program, "Developing the total brain" [accessed October 1, 2010], http://www.tm.org/benefits-brain.

18. Harung, Travis, Blank, and Heaton, "Higher Development, Brain Integration, and Excellence in Leadership," 872-894.

Chapter 17: Self-Empowerment and Women's Liberation

1. Maharishi, *Bhagavad Gita: A New Translation and Commentary*, 210. (4:22)

2. Miranda Koerner, "More women graduate from college," http://www.mysanantonio.com/community/northwest/news/article/More-women-graduate-from-college-793606.php.

3. A. Towfighi, L. Zheng, and B. Ovbiagele, "Sex-Specific Trends in Midlife Coronary Heart Disease Risk and Prevalence," *Archives of Internal Medicine* 169(19)(2009), 1762-1766. http://www.ncbi. nlm.nih.gov/pubmed/19858433

4. *Scientific Research on the Maharishi Transcendental Meditation and TM-Sidhi Programs: A Brief Summary of 500 Studies,* 14.

Chapter 18: Mother Divine—The Divine Feminine

1. Maharishi Lecture, December 31, 1970, Poland Springs, Maine, USA.

2. For more information on:
The Mother Divine Program, see www.motherdivine.org
The Maharishi Purusha program, see www.purusha.org.

Chapter 19: World Peace

1. Quoted in Oates, *Permanent Peace,* 198.

2. Quoted in Abell, *Talks with Great Composers,* xiv.

3. Quoted in Pearson, *The Complete Book of Yogic Flying,* 459.

4. Quoted in Pearson, *The Complete Book of Yogic Flying,* 459.

5. DrMartinLutherKingJr.com. "Audios and Text of His Most Famous Speeches and Writings," http://www.drmartinluther kingjr.com.

6. Federal Bureau of Investigations, "Latest Crime Statistics: Volumes Continue to Fall," http://www.fbi.gov/news/stories/ 2011/september/crime_091911/crime_091911.

The Huffington Post, "LA's Crime Rate Lowest In 50 Years," http://www.huffingtonpost.com/2010/01/06/las-crime-rate-lo west-in-_n_413760.html.

Bureau of Justice Statistics, "Violent Crime Rate Trends," http://bjs.ojp.usdoj.gov/content/glance/tables/viortrdtab.cfm.

7. Carla Johnson, "ADHD In Children: PESTICIDES May Be Missing Link," http://www.huffingtonpost.com/2010/05/17/adhd-pesticides-in-fruits_n_578366.html.

8. *Scientific Research on the Maharishi Transcendental Meditation and TM-Sidhi Programs: A Brief Summary of 500 Studies*, 21-23.

9. Pearson, *The Complete Book of Yogic Flying*, 64-65.

10. For more information on the Global Peace Initiative, a brain-based approach to reducing violence and global conflict, visit www.globalpeaceinitiative.org.

Chapter 20: Heaven on Earth

1. Oates, *Celebrating the Dawn*, cover.

2. Global Good News, "Scintillating Intelligence - 02 March 2012," http://www.globalgoodnews.com/scintillating-intelligence-arch ive/24.html.

3. CBS News, "Popping Pills a Popular Way to Boost Brain Power," http://www.cbsnews.com/stories/2010/04/22/60minutes/mai n6422159.shtml.

4. For more information visit: www.davidlynchfoundation.org

5. For more information visit: www.maharishischooliowa.org

6. Paul Hawken, *Blessed Unrest: How the Largest Movement in the World Came into Being and Why No One Saw it Coming* (New York: Penguin Group, 2007).

7. MAIL FOREIGN SERVICE, "Plastic paradise: Scientists plan to turn Pacific Ocean waste into a floating island," http://www.dailymail.co.uk/news/article-1290525/Plastic-para dise-Scientists-plan-turn-Pacific-Ocean-waste-floating-island.html.

8. For more information visit: http://givingpledge.org.

9. *Maharishi's Master Plan to Create Heaven on Earth* (The Netherlands: Maharishi Vedic University Press, 1991), 4.

Conclusion

1. GoodReads.com, "Amelia Earhart Quotes," http://www.goodreads.com/author/quotes/367092.Amelia_Earhart

FOR MORE INFORMATION

www.enlightenmentforeveryone.com

- The Transcendental Meditation technique and how to learn:
  www.tm-women.org

- Programs for women and the ladies' wing of the
  Transcendental Meditation organization:
  www.tmwomenprofessionals.org
  www.globalwomensorganization.org
  www.globalhealthfoundationforwomen.org

- Maharishi University of Enlightenment, which offers degree
  programs for ladies:
  www.maharishiuniversityofenlightenment.com

- The Mother Divine Program:
  www.motherdivine.org

- Maharishi University of Management:
  www.mum.edu

- Maharishi School of the Age of Enlightenment:
  www.maharishischooliowa.org

- The David Lynch Foundation for Consciousness-Based
  Education and World Peace:
  www.davidlynchfoundation.org

- News of positive trends rising in the world:
  www.globalgoodnews.com

- The Global Peace Initiative:
  www.globalpeaceinitiative.org

RECOMMENDED READING

- *Science of Being and Art of Living—Transcendental Meditation* by Maharishi Mahesh Yogi

- *Maharishi Mahesh Yogi on the Bhagavad-Gita: A New Translation and Commentary, Chapters 1-6* by Maharishi Mahesh Yogi

- *The TM Book: How to Enjoy the Rest of Your Life* by Denise Denniston

- *Transcendental Meditation* by Bob Roth

- *Transcendence: Healing and Transformation through Transcendental Meditation* by Dr. Norman Rosenthal

- *Catching the Big Fish: Meditation, Consciousness, and Creativity* by David Lynch

- *The Neurophysiology of Enlightenment* by Dr. Robert Keith Wallace

ABOUT THE AUTHOR

Ann Purcell has been a full-time teacher of Transcendental Meditation since 1973, teaching Transcendental Meditation and advanced courses in many countries around the world. In addition, she has worked on curricula and course development for universities and continuing education programs. She has a B.SCI (Bachelor of the Science of Creative Intelligence) and an M.SCI from Maharishi European Research University, Seelisberg, Switzerland. She also received a PhD in Supreme Political Science from Maharishi University of World Peace, Vlodrop, Netherlands. She is the author of *Tender Flower of Heaven*, a collection of 120 poems, and also writes for the Huffington Post.

CONNECT

Questions? Comments? Ann Purcell can be contacted online at:
www.enlightenmentforeveryone.com/contact/

Read more blog posts about enlightenment, health, world peace, etc:
www.enlightenmentforeveryone.com/blog
www.huffingtonpost.com/ann-purcell/

Facebook: www.facebook.com/Enlightenmentforeveryone
Twitter: www.twitter.com/purcell_ann
Youtube: www.youtube.com/enlightenmentbook

OTHER BOOKS

BY GREEN DRAGON

- *The Tao of Leadership*
  by John Heider

- *The Tao Te Ching–A New Approach: Backward Down the Path*
  by Jerry O. Dalton

- *Insight Outlook*
  by Dr. Albert Hofmann

- *The Tao of Recovery: A Quiet Path to Wellness*
  by Jim McGregor

- *The Tao of Calm: 81 Meditations for Everyday Living*
  by Pamela Metz

CPSIA information can be obtained
at www.ICGtesting.com
Printed in the USA
FFHW010045050419
51467301-56912FF